St. James Parish Register

[Baltimore County, Maryland]

1787–1815

COMPILED BY

Bill AND *Martha Reamy*

HERITAGE BOOKS
2019

HERITAGE BOOKS

AN IMPRINT OF HERITAGE BOOKS, INC.

Books, CDs, and more—Worldwide

For our listing of thousands of titles see our website
at
www.HeritageBooks.com

Published 2019 by
HERITAGE BOOKS, INC.
Publishing Division
5810 Ruatan St.
Berwyn Heights, MD 20740

International Standard Book Numbers
Paperbound: 978-1-58549-102-5
Clothbound: 978-0-7884-6927-5

ST. JAMES PARISH

Today the church of St. James of My Lady's Manor stands near the intersection of Monkton and Old York Roads, near modern real estate developments. When the church was first built, starting in 1752, it stood in the rolling country, barely settled, near what would become the border of Baltimore and Harford Counties. Jennie E. Jessop, writing in the December 1968 issue of History Trails, states that the church was first planned as a chapel of ease in 1750, designed to save some of the parishioners of St. John's Parish a long ride to church. This chapel comprises the nave of the present day church.

As with many modern buildings, construction costs exceeded the original estimates and in 1754 and 1755 an additional £70,000 was levied on the taxables of the parish to complete construction. The original windows of bubble glass have been replaced by stained glass memorial windows. Twelve of the original pews, installed in the 1750's, still remain, and the appointments of the interior include a number of altar frontals made in England, a set of vestments from Canada, and an eighteenth century set of Nativity figures from Italy.

Until 1777 the chapel was a part of St. John's Parish, but in January of the latter year it became an independent parish. In March 1779 Reverend George Hughes Worsley was called to be the first rector. He was to divide his time between the parishes of St.John's and St. James. There are no vestry records or registers of birth, death, and marriage dating from his tenure, but we know that in May 1780 the Vestry of St. James wrote to the Vestry of St. John's requesting that Reverend Worsley attend St. James' services on the fourth Sunday of each month. He also gave one Sunday a month to Mr. Hunter's chapel in the St. John's Parish, and the other two Sundays to preaching at St. John's. According to the parish history, St. James of My Lady's Manor, 1750-1950, the work of serving the three pulpits was so heavy that by the end of 1780 he left for Charles County where he served the Port Tobacco Parish.

The second rector was the Reverend John Andrews who served from 1782 to 1785. He was a member of the first graduating class from the College of Philadelphia (fore-runner of the University of Pennsylvania), and later taught at an academy in York, Pennsylvania. A distinguished classical scholar, he divided his time between St. James and St. Thomas Parishes. In April 1785 Reverend Andrews took his family back to Philadelphia where he devoted the remainder of his life to teaching.

For two years the church was again without a rector, and then in July 1787 Reverend John Coleman, a native of Virginia, was called as the third rector. He served until 1816, and at one time served three parishes (St. James, St. Thomas, and one other) simultaneously. During his pastorate the registers of birth, death, and marriage were preserved, the first Vestry minutes have been recorded, and his personal diary contains a number of entries pertaining to the lives of his parishioners.

The original register containing marriages, 1787-1814, and births and christenings, 1783-1815, is now at the Maryland Historical Society in the Manuscript Division (MS.720). This register was recopied by Lucy H. Harrison, and placed in the Library of the Historical Society. In the back of this transcript are several pages of typed entries from Reverend Coleman's diary, noting the dates of death, names, and ages of a number of the people whose funerals he conducted. Some later records of a nineteenth century rector, Rev. John Reeder Keech, have been published in the Bulletin of the Maryland Genealogical Society, vol. 19, no. 3, pp. 158-161.

The church is surrounded on four sides by some of the oldest tombstones in the county. Many of these were copied and published in Ridgely's Historic Graves of Maryland and Delaware. More recently the older section of the graveyard was copied by members of the Historical and Genealogical Societies of Baltimore County.

This publication contains the entries found in the volume kept by Reverend Coleman.

In compiling this work, Mrs. Reamy used both the transcript by Lucy H. Harrison and the original volume at the manuscript department of the Maryland Historical Society.

Robert Barnes

* * * * *

ABBREVIATIONS

B · married by bann   HC -- Harford County
BC - Baltimore County   L - married by license
FC Frederick County

```
1787
AUG  5    William FORD & Lucy JAMES - BC, St. James
     31    John GRAYHAM & Mary MCGAWLEY - FC
SEP 11    Bond James KIMBOLEY & Mary MILLS - HC
     11    John MOORES & Mary LEE - HC
OCT 18    Edmond STANDEFORD & Hannah GRAY - FC
     30    John Holt GUYTON & Sarah WATKINS - BC
NOV 13    Godfrey WATERS & Martha BRADFORD  - FC
DEC  6    John CROMWELL & Urarth OWINGS  - BC
     18    Dennis MCLAUGHLIN & Mary DAWSON  - BC

1788
JAN  1    Thomas CHINWORTH & Rachel NORRIS -  FC
FEB 28    Michael CRAWS & Sarah HANSON  - FC
MAR 23    William GWYNN & Eleanor CAMPBELL  - BC
     25    Benjamin JONES & Sarah JONES  - BC
APR  6    Richard WARD & Martha BEWARD - FC
MAY  4    Peter HOLDING & Sarah HAIR  - HC
     12    Thomas WORREL & Mary CONDEN - BC
JUNE 1    Henry RUFF & Anna PRESTON  - FC
      2    Benjamin SEDGWICK & Mary ALBERT - FC
     25    William STEWARD & Elizabeth GUYTON - BC
JULY 1    John GREEN & Cassandra SMITHSON - PC
     17    Peter BOWLER & Rachel COEN - HC
OCT  2    Benjamin DOWNS & Blanch HAMPTON - FC
     28    Abraham JONES & Mary GITTINGS - BC
NOV 13    Samuel HICKERSON & Mary THRAP - HC
     19    Martin RENSHAW - BC & Magdaline JONES - FC
     28    John BURNET & Hannah SPENCER - FC
DEC 25    Thomas NASH & Lucretia WEEKS - FC
     28    Andrew BURNS & Mary BUSSEY - FC

1789
JAN  1    Thomas DUNSTON & Ann LIGET - BC
      4    William LEE & Margaret DAY - HC
     29    Nathan PHIPPS & Rebecca DAVIES - PC, St. Johns
FEB  2    Richard TAYLOR & Clemency THOMSON - FC, St. Johns
      8    Emanuel REED & Ann HUNT - FC, St. Johns
     22    James STEWARD & Eleanor DYNES - FC
     22    James HUDSON & Dorothea BATTEN - PC
APR 14    John NEAL & Mary SCOFIELD - BC
MAY  7    Elijah BOSLEY - BC & Hannah WILMOT - FC
     10    Charles HIPKINS & Elizabeth MYRES - BC
JUNE 7    James MONTGOMERY & Susanna WHITAKER - FC
     16    Josias WHEELER & Martha PRIGG - FC
AUG 13    James MULLOY & Sarah WEEKS - FC
SEP 10    George RIGBY & Eleanor SMITH - BC
     10    John MASON & Ann CONDON
     20    John NORTON & Sarah JONES - St. Johns
     27    William ARVIN & Elizabeth HARDCASTLE
```

ST. JAMES MARRIAGES

1789

SEP 27	Robert PEAK & Elizabeth MURRY - St. Johns
OCT 20	Abraham HILTON & Elizabeth GRIMES - St. Johns, BC
NOV 12	Edward KELLY & Delilah POCOCK - BC
12	Thomas GIBSON - HC & Eliza BOND - St. James, BC
17	Fredrick MCCOMAS & Susanna ONION - FC
21	Isaac GUYTON & Margaret HETHORN - FC
DEC 24	Lucas GILLAM & Temperance CORBIN - FC

1790

JAN 7	William BAGLEY & Susanna HUSBANDS - FC
FEB 2	John ROCKHOLD & Martha WATERS - HC
11	William RICHARDSON & Mary MORGAN - FC
18	George PATRICK & Ruth MONTGOMERY - FC
25	Thomas Sheredine CHEW & Elizabeth MORGAN - FC
MAR 15	Robert TURNBULL- Va. & Sarah BUCKANAN - BC
APR 3	Henry NORRIS & Margaret GORDEN - HC
25	William MACKBEE - BC & Jamima GROVER - HC
MAY 2	Henry BYFORD & Mary MCCLURE - BC
11	Thomas CORBIN & Nancy TURNER - St. Johns, HC
18	Daniel RAWLEY & Mary ROBB - St. Johns
20	John HAMBLETON & Phebe MAXWELL - HC
JUNE 27	Robert ALEXANDER & Rebecca HAYS - FC
AUG 15	Henry DOWNS & Deleah ENLOWS - BC
SEP 5	James GALLOWAY & Mary CHINE - St. Johns, BC
12	Aquila SAMSON & Mary INLOWS - St. James, BC
30	Jesse HOLLINGSWORTH & Rachel Lyde PARKIN - BC-L
OCT 7	William GOE- BC & Cassandra JONES - HC - L BC
21	Nathaniel NICHOLAS & Elizabeth HARRIS - HC - L
NOV 18	William GRANT & Catharine HOLLAND - HC - B
DEC 14	John MERRYMAN & Sarah JOHNSON - BC - L
23	William MAGNESS & Sarah WATERS - HC - B
26	George COLLINS & Sarah BAYLEY - BC - L
27	Thomas CROUCH & Elizabeth MCGOWAN - HC - L

1791

JAN 13	James FULLERTON & Sarah BRADFORD - HC - L
FEB 15	Benjamin VANHORN & Charity SANDERS - FC - B
20	Thomas DURHAM & Rachel SHOUDY - FC - B
27	Henry ENLOWS & Nancy SAMPSON - BC - B
MAR 15	Charles COLEMAN & Lydia FORWOOD - FC - L
17	Thomas WRIGHT & Ann GREEN - FC - L
24	Nathan BAKER & Belinda BOSLEY - BC - L
28	Ephraim DONAVAN & Charlotte TAYLOR
MAY 15	Leonard COWEN & Mary FOWLER - St. Johns - L
29	Thomas ROCK & Rebecca REED - St. Johns - B
JUNE 23	John BRANNIAN & Sarah GEORGE - FC - L
JULY 12	George DEBRULER & Aminta NUTTERWELL - FC - L
24	Thomas WALTER & Ann DELANY - BC - B
AUG 21	Kid LYNCH & Sarah SWARTH - St. Johns - B
12	John WRIGHT & Rebecca OTHARSON - St. Johns - L
25	William WALSH & Blanch LEE - HC - L
30	Peter LONG & Margaret CARR - HC - L
SEP 11	James WEAR & Charity KEY - St. Johns - FC - B

```
1791
SEPT 26    Isaac LOW & Jemima HITCHCOCK - HC - L
OCT 2      David ASQUITH & Frances NICHOLS - BC- L issued  HC
NOV 20     Salathiel TUDER & Temperance FUGATE - BC- L issued BC
DEC 22     Thomas BOND & Ann TALBOTT - BC - L
   27      John MCCUBBIN & Polley TUDER - BC - St. Johns - L
   27      Asael BARTON & Susannah MILLIKIN - BC - St. Johns-L

1792
JAN 12     Josias JOHNSON & Peggy MORGAN - FC - L
   25      Arthur' LONGDAN & Mary LEWIS - FC - L
   26      John WILLIAMS & Rachel VAUGHAN - BC - L
FEB 2      Enoch CHURCHMAN & Martha NORRIS - FC -L issued HC
   12      George ELLENDER & Sarah GRIMES - BC - L
   16      Henry Bateman GOE & Susanna GITTINGS - BC - L
   21      Henry WATERS & Grace WILSON - HC - L
MAR 1      Benjamin PARISH & Nancy HUNTER - BC - L
    4      Aquila GALLOWAY & Ann BARTON - BC - L
   11      Zacharias DURHAM & Lucia HUSBAND - HC - B
   13      John HUGHES & Elizabeth GUDGEON - BC - L
   22      John MAGAW - BC & Sarah HUTCHINS - HC - L issued BC
   22      Maurice MAULSBY & Eleanor MAULSBY - HC - L
APR 15     Charles ROCKHOLD & Eleanor POCOCK - HC - L
   23      Peter John ROBERTS & Maria SANDERSONS - HC - L
   26      Henry Patrick FINNAGAN & Aranca SLEMAKER - HC - L
JUN 17     Thomas JOHNSON-HC & Elizabeth CORD-BC-St. Johns-
           L - issued BC
   19      Samuel MCMATH & Mary CURRY - HC - St. Johns - B
   21      Anthony LYNCH & Mary BARTON - BC - L
AUG 1      Jesse MATTHEWS & Ann CONN - HC - L
   23      Daniel NORRIS & Frances HUGHS - HC - L
   27      Arnold RUSH & Jane CONN - HC - L issued 25th
OCT 9      Joshua TUDER & Susanna MCCUBBINS - BC - St. Johns - L-
           issued 6th.
   11      John ADDISON, Jr. & Sarah LERTCH - BCo-L issued BC
   21      Francis CARTY & Magdalene JUEL - HC - St. Johns - B
NOV 6      Joshua ADY & Mary FORD - HC&BC - L issued HC - St.Johns
    6      Lambert SMITH & Elizabeth GITTINGS - BC -St. Johns - L
   11      Joshua RUTLEDGE & Augustine BIDDEL - BC - L
   12      John MCCRACKEN & Sarah SMITH - HC - L
DEC 4      William Wilkinson WAITS & Susanna STANSBURY - BC - L
   11      William MCMATH & Sarah MOORES - HC - St. Johns - L
   13      Jacob FULKS & Priscilla PURKINS - BC - St. Johns - B
   25      James WOODLAND & Sarah COLLINS - HC - St. Johns - B
   25      Benjamin CARROLL & Milly PROCTON - HC - St. Johns - B
   27      Moses TAYLOR & Nancy DURBAN - HC - St. Johns - B
   29      Richard BUTLER & Sarah BOTTS - HC - L

1793
JAN 1      Daniel MOORES & Sarah BUDD - HC - L
   18      Michael NIGER & Sarah MORGAN - HC - L
   27      William ROACH & Elizabeth HAMBLETON - HC -St. Johns - B
   31      Ephraim Gittings GOVER & Elisabeth GOVER -HC-St.Johns-L
FEB 7      John LUCAS & Sarah DWINS (?) - BC - St. Johns - L
```

1793

FEB 17	Gabriel HOLMES & Mary BACON - BC - St. James - L
17	Isaac BOSLEY & Elizabeth HUTCHINS - BC -St. James - L
MAR 3	Nicholas PARISH & Elizabeth JOHNSON - BC - St. James - L
APR 2	Thomas Gassaway HOWARD & Martha Susanne TALLY- BC - L
14	Thomas WINGATE -HC & Sarah POTTEE - B or HC -St. James- L issued HC
MAY 2	Bazil BOSLEY & Rebecca CHAMBERLIN - BC - L
28	Willilam DUKE & Hester CONDON - CC - L
JUN 2	Thomas WELCH & Martha GROVES - HC - L
17	John HAMBLETON & Peggy BOND- HC - L
30	John STRICKLAND & Alice PERRY- HC - St. Johns - B
JULY 23	Charles HOPKINS - HC & Ann JENKINS - BC - L issued HC
29	Thomas BROWN & Hannah MURRY - BC - St. Johns - B
SEP 15	John MIDDLETON & Mary COWAN - HC -St. Johns - L iss. BC
29	James MURRY & Susanne SWANN - St. James - B
NOV 3	John BOWERS & Hannah BRONWELL - HC - L
7	Thomas SADLER & Elisabeth HOWARD - BC - L
19	John BUCK & Catharine MERRYMAN - BC - L
21	Samuel WALLIS & Cassandra JOLLEY - HC - L
30	Andrew STEVINSON & Isabella SMITH - HC -L
DEC 10	Moses MAXWELL & Salley Charity BOND - HC - L
26	Isaac LEADLEY & Nancey MACKUBBINS - BC - St. Johns - L
29	Edward DAWS & Ann GRUNDEN - HC - L

1794

JAN 5	Thomas RUTLEDGE & Ann BURTON - BC - St. James - B
FEB 16	Peter DELEVET & Ann JONES - BC - St. Johns - L
MAR 25	John Ridgely NICHOLSON & Matilda Heath SMITH- BC-L
27	Dickinson GORSUCH & Mary TALBOTT - BC - L
APR 6	Thomas FERRELL & Ruth GALLOWAY - BC - B
MAY 22	Thomas JOHNSON & Anne GILES - BC - L
29	James MCCOMAS & Sarah HOWARD - HC - L
JUN 5	John MARCHE & Hannah ONION - HC - St. James - L
29	Francis HARE & Mary GALOWAY - BC - St. James - L issued HC 6/25
JUL 20	John LITTLE & Elisabeth ADAMS - St. Johns - B
24	Nicholas Day MCCOMAS & Elisabeth ONION-HC-L iss. 7/23
27	James HALL & Elisabeth CONNOLLY - HC - St. James - B
AUG 26	David POCOCK & Mary SMITH - BC -L issued HC 8/14
SEP 23	Patrick DONNELL & Margaret BRYCE - St. George - B
OCT 28	Paul Airnee (?) FLEURY & Clara YOUNG - BC - L
NOV 15	John CLARK & Cassandra ANDERSON - HC - L
20	James DALL & Sarah Brooke HOLLIDAY - BC - L
DEC 23	Hosea JOHNS & Penelope SLADE - BC - L
30	James GIVEN & Elisabeth GREEN - BC - L

1795

JAN 29	Thomas TALBOTT & Elisabeth RUTLEDGE - BC - L
FEB 5	Henry DORSEY of Edwd. & Elisabeth SMITHSON, HC - L
19	William ELLENOR & Barbara BEMER - BC - L
MAR 5	Joseph SCOTT - BC & Hannah NORRIS - HC - L issued BC
29	William EVERIT & Sarah COOPER - St. Johns - B
APR 9	Henry WILSON & Sarah WORTHINGTON - St. Johns-L iss. BC

4

```
1795
MAY 21      Thomas WALTHAM & Martha GREENFIELD - HC - L
     24     George SPEAR & Catharine RENNER - BC - B
JUL  5      John LAURENCE & Rebecca YARLEY - St. Johns - B
DEC 10      William ASKEW & Sarah CALWELL - St. Johns - L iss. BC
     17     Richard GOTT & Ruth BAILEY -BC - L
     24th   Ralph YARLEY? & Ruth BURTON - St. Johns-L issued BC

1796
JAN 10      Charles JOHNSON & Mary FUGATE - BC -L
FEB  2      Robert WHITEFORD & Nancy MCCAIRNAN - HC - L -St. James
            or St. Johns
     18     Daniel MCCOMAS & Elisabeth SCOTT - HC - L
JUN  2      John WATKINS & Ruth GUYTON - BC - L
SEP  1      William DIMMITT & Nancy TRAPNALL - BC - L
OCT  4      James HUNTER & Jemima INLOES  - BC - L
      4     Mordicai BOND & Hannah HUGHES - St. James-L issued BC
NOV 17      Thomas JOHNSON & Elisabeth TAYLOR - HC - L
     17     Bryan PHILPOT & Elisabeth JOHNSON - BC - L

1797
JAN 19      Zaccheus Onion BOND & Cassandra Lee MORGAN, HC - L
     26     John HAMBLETON & Aley GAFFORD - HC - L
FEB 19      Robert GWYNN & Elizabeth GWYNN - BC - L
MAR  9      Thomas SHEREDINE & Ann NEILL - HC - L
APR  6      Daniel SCOTT & Margaret SHORT - HC - L
MAY  2      Henry WEATHERALL & Charlotte E. DAY - HC - L
     18     John QUARLES - Va & Elisabeth HUSBANDS - HC - L
     25     Francis HOLLAND & Sybel WEST - BC - L
JUN 29      James ST. CLAIR & Susanna BOSLEY - L issued HC
JUL 22      William GODMAN & Deliah WHITE - L issued HC
     27     Henry O. HENRY & Ann PRICE - HC - L
AUG  3      John MOORE & Mary SCARBROUGH - HC - L
      8     Richard TYDINGS & Susanna CHAMBERLAIN - BC - L
      8     James SMITH & Sarah HALEY - HC - L
SEP 21      William WEATHERALL & Mary PRESBURY - HC - L
     21     Parker GILBERT & Martha MCCOMAS - HC - L
OCT 19      Daniel CUNNINGHAM & Anna AMOSS - HC - L
NOV  2      William NEILL & Mary SHEREDINE - HC - L
     23     Ruthen GARRISON & Mary GALLION - HC - L
DEC  7      William LINAM & Sarah PINIX - HC - L issued  12/5
      7     Thomas BIRKHEAD & Elisabeth WATERS - L issued BC
     18     Thomas STOCKDALE & Sarah BAXTER - HC - L issued 12/18

1798
JAN 25      Morgan JONES & Cordelia BAKER - HC -L 1/24
FEB  8      Charles KINZIL & Ann JOHNSON - HC - L 2/8
MAR  2      William Lee WILSON & Sarah Chew LEE - HC - L iss. 2/28
APR 19      John HOPKINS & Eleanor MORGAN - HC - L iss. 4/16
JUN  7      James WHITE & Hannah BULL - HC - L
     26     Nicholas MERRYMAN of Benj. & Sarah ANDERSON - BC
AUG 16      Matthew DENISON & Sarah SHEARWOOD - HC
     23     Joseph JAMES & Elisabeth SHEARWOOD
OCT  9      Samuel VANCE & Mary WATTERS - HC - L
DEC 11      Edward Aquila HOWARD & Charlotte RUMSEY- HC - St. Johns
```

ST. JAMES MARRIAGES

1799
JAN 17	Clement MARSH & Jemima ELLIOT - BC - St. James
MAR 13	Archibald GITTINGS & Elisabeth BOSLEY - BC - St. James
APR 18	Joseph HOPKINS & Sarah MORGAN - HC - St. Georges
30	Philip MOORE & Deliah HALL - BC - St. Johns
MAY 2	Nathan HORNER & Delia CARROLL - HC - St. Johns
16	Peter HOOFMAN-St. Thomas & Deborah OWINGS-BC-St.Thomas
JUN 23	William JACKSON & Mary BLAYDON - St. Thomas
SEP 26	James HUTCHINGS & Margaret GIVEN - BC - St. James
OCT 16	William THORN & Sarah SATER - BC - L - St. Thomas
NOV 6	James BOSLEY & Hannah HUGHES - BC - L - St. James

1800
FEB 6	Richard CROMWELL - AC & Mary OWINGS - BC - St. Thomas dated 2/5
MAR 25	Basil SOLLERS & Susanna OWINGS - St. Thomas
AUG 7	George TORNQUIST & Anna Margaretha ELKINS -BC-St. James
OCT 14	Robert DOWNY & Rachel SOTHERLAND - BC - St. Thomas
NOV 16	William Bois HINES & Elizabeth LAWRENCE, the former of Kentucky, the latter of BC - St. Thomas

1801
JAN 11	Job CHAPMAN & Ann SYKES - BC - St. Thomas
JUL 2	Robert North MOALE & Frances OWINGS - BC - St. Thomas
NOV 5	Matthew STACY & Jane FLETCHER - BC - St. Thomas-L 10/31
26	Joseph SHEETZ & Ruth OWINGS - BC - St. Thomas

1801
DEC 10	Thomas GITTINGS & Mary WILMOT-BC-St. Pauls or St. Thomas

1802
FEB 9	Richard JOHNSON - FC & Eleanor JOHNSON - BC - St. James
APR 27	Edward RUTLEDGE & Susanna WILSON - BC - St. James
MAY 27	John YEISER & Eleanor A. HOLLIDAY -BC - St. Thomas
JUNE 10	Samuel STUMP & Martha Burrows STONE - St. Thomas
AUG 8	Adam SHIPLEY & Ruth CRISMAN - BC - St. Thomas
DEC 16	Nicholas MERRYMAN of Elijah & Charlotte WORTHINGTON-BC - St. Thomas

1803
MAR 1	Charles WORTHINGTON & Susanna JOHNS - BC - St. Thomas
22	John SLADE & Elisabeth HUTCHINGS - HC - St. James
APR 19	Robert MAXWELL & Elizabeth ROGERS - BC - St. James
AUG 11	Thomas Beale OWINGS & Ann JOHNSON - BC - St. Pauls

1804
JAN 29	Thomas TALBOTT & Mary MERRYMAN - BC - St. James
FEB 21	William WILMER & Anna FORD - St. Johns
APR 10	Oswald JENKINS & Sarah PEARCE - BC - St. James
17	Isaac HOLLINGSWORTH & Cassandra DIVERS - St. Johns
JUN 21	Walter CUNNINGHAM & Cassandra LUCK - St. George
AUG 2	John WILIE & Ann RICKETS - St. George or St. James
DEC 20	William NELSON & Hannah HUTCHINGS - St. James

```
1805
JAN 1      Thomas B. DORSEY & Sarah WORTHINGTON - St. Thomas
    8      Fayette JOHNSON & Elisabeth CRADOCK - St. Thomas
   10      John KERNS & Mary ELLIOTT - St. James
   24      Jesse HUTCHINGS & Jemmima GALLOWAY - St. James
APR 18
  18th     John SHEREDINE & Ann ALLEN - HC - St. Johns
JUL 25     Thomas RAINE & Charlotte CRAVEN - HC - St. Johns
NOV 21     William EWING & Elisabeth NORRINGTON - St. Johns

1806
FEB 9      Israel D. MAULSBY & Jane HALL - HC - St. Johns
   27      Thomas CARR & Milcah MERRYMAN - St. James
MAR 27     Edward HAMBLETON & Priscilla JOHNSON - HC
APR 6      Thomas DEMOSS & Sarah RANDALL - St. James
   17      Charles WORTHINGTON & Hannah YELLOTT - HC - St. Johns
   24      James BEATY & Catharine DEMOSS - St. James
MAY 1      John YELLOTT & Rebecca R. COLEMAN - HC - St. Johns
           by Rev'd. John Allen

1809
FEB 2      James FULTON & Hannah AMOS - HC - St. James
MAR 30     Isaac ATKINSON & Hannah BURNET - HC - St. Johns or St.
           James
APR 23     Bennet LOVE & Elisabeth GILBERT - HC - Christ Church
JULY 27    William BAILY & Rachel PRESTON - HC - Christ Church
AUG 17     Henry LONG & Eliza Ann GITTINGS - BC - St. John or
           St.James
SEP 28     Moses ST. CLAIR & Ann BLANEY -St. James or Christ Church
OCT 12     Brice John WORTHINGTON & Ann Lee FITZHUGH - St. James

1810
JAN 7      John STANDIFORD & Delea HUTCHINGS - St. James
FEB ?      Andrew WILSON & Rebecca SCARFF - St. James

1811
FEB 21     Joshua KELSO & Sarah HUTCHINS - St. James

1812
JAN 16     Ralph LEE & Elisabeth SMITHSON - HC
SEP ?      Vincent Jeoffrey WATKINS & Elisabeth ALDRIDGE - HC
OCT 8      William GRIFFIN & Amelia MAGNESS - HC
NOV 12     Joshua DAY & Sarah DAWNEY - HC
   17      Lloyd STANDIFORD & Mary HINDON - HC

1813
FEB        Thomas STREET & Catharine MERRYMAN - BC - St. James
   ?       Joshua HENDRICK & Sarah GALLOWAY - St. James
DEC 13     John JORDAN & Rachel FULTON
   23      Robert ALLEN & Elisabeth HOPKINS - HC

1814
OCT 18     Thomas ELY & Ann Maria LANCASTER
```

7

PERSONS CONFIRMED AT THE MANOR CHURCH (?) ST. JAMES
SEPTEMBER 5TH 1795
by BISHOP CLEGGETT

George FITZHUGH; Mary FITZHUGH; George FITZHUGH, Jr.; Daniel
FITZHUGH; Grafton BELT; Cornelius GARRISON; Susanna GARRISON;
Mary NICHOLSON; Mary NICHOLSON; Charles Ridgely NICHOLSON;
Charles ROCKHOLD; Eleanor ROCKHOLD; Sarah GARRISON; Ann GARRISON;
Sarah GALLOWAY; John STEWART; Ruth BLANEY; Ann GUYTON; Elizabeth
ROGERS; Sarah POCOCK; Ann KNIGHT; Matilda HUTCHINGS; Mary AIRS;
Ephraim RUTLIDGE; Delea HUTCHINGS; NEGRO JACK

by REV. JOHN COLEMAN

PARENTS' NAMES	CHILDREN'S NAMES	BORN
Parker & Elisabeth LEE	William Dellam	1785
William & Agnes MOREN	Jenney	1783
	Thomas	1786
George & Unity JOHNSON	James	1786
Aaron & Elizabeth GORDON	Elizabeth	1786
Robert & Martha MORGAN	Thomas John Hamilton	1785
Joseph & Margaret TOWNSLEY	John (Joseph*)	1786

* Added later in different handwriting.

Robert & Ann JINKINS	Sarah	1785
William & Mary CATREL	William Regden	—
Benjamin & ___	Milcah	—
James & ___ HUGHS	Margaret	—
Alexander & Elizabeth STEWARD	John	8/7/1787
John & Pleasance COLEMAN	Charles Ridgely	4/17/1786
	Rebecca R.	8/8/1787
	John	12/15/1788
	Samuel Jarratt	6/1/1791
	Samuel Williamson	2/9/1793
	Curthbert William	9/8/1794
Joshua & Jane MILES	John	
Edward & Jane SWAIN	Rachel	8/8/1787
Abraham & Ann GUITON	Joshua	6/9/1787
Thomas & Rachel SLADE	Zale	6/9/1787
Thomas & Mary RICHARDSON	Ruth	
John & Frances PERRY	Samuel	— 1786
William & Ann PERRY	William	1787
	Sarah	7/8/1788
Thomas & Mary STROUD	Elizabeth	1785
	Rachel	1787
Francis & ___ SPARK	Penelope	1/27/1787
___ & Mary STROUD	Harriett	6/1/1787
Lester SYNCLEAR & ___	Elizabeth	3/25/1787
Thomas & Ann HUNT	Mary	3/22/1787
James & Sarah RAMPLEY	James	10/25/1786
Robert & Sarah BRYARLY	David	7/26/1785
	Thomas	8/15/1787
John & Rachel WHITAKER	Joshua Johnson	8/5/1779
Jacob & Mary HALL	Thomas Parry	12/21/1789
	bapt.	11/30/1791
Joshua & Sarah BUCK	Chloe	12/1/1790
Nathan & Rachel ANDERSON	John	12/23/1782
	Joshua	2/5/1785
Hannah COOP/James COOP her ba. sponsor	William	4/27/1790
Jacob & Sarah BULL	Mary	10/9/1780
	Margaret	3/14/1791
John & Martha LEE	James	11/16/1791
Zephaniah & Abby TOLBY (TOLLEY ?)	Elizabeth	5/14/1791
Joseph & Elizabeth HUNTER	Joseph	8/30/1791
Robert & Mary MORGAN	William Groom	2/25/1790

9

Parents	Child	Birth Date
Abraham & Ann GUYTON	William	7/4/1789
	Isaac	11/2/1791
Lyde & Abby GOODWIN	Elizabeth	10/11/1790
	Thomas Parkin	10/4/1791
Richard & Rachel COOLEY	Mehaly	2/16/1791
William & Sarah TRONER	Jane	3/2/1791
Benjamin & Elisabeth RODES	John	3/12/1791
Robert & Sarah BRYARLY	James	4/13/1791
James & Mary ASHTON	James	5/11/1792
Edward & Eleanor ELIOTT	William	1/3/1788
	Samuel	8/12/1790
	Sarah	2/1/1792
Benjamin & Salina SEDGWICK	John	11/7/1791
John & Frances PERRY	Henry	10/6/1791
James & Lurana KELLEY	Unity	10/28/1791
William & Ann PERRY	Susanna	10/1/1790
John & Mary PRIGG	Elizabeth	1/6/1792
Joseph & Elizabeth CARLIN	Robert	2/15/1792
John & Elizabeth WARD	Margaret	2/2/1784
	Martha	10/29/1789
Samuel CORBET & Martha ANDERSON	Jesse	3/9/1787
Abraham & Mary HAMMOND	James Dickinson	6/15/1791
Bazzel & Sarah WALLER	Mary	12/20/1791
_____ & Margaret GERMAN	Walter Presbury	12/5/1791
John & Elizabeth THOMSON	Moses	11/15/1790
Isaac & Rebecca GREEN	Charles	1/31/1792
Milor LEGET	Jessee	12/11/1791
James & Cassandra HAYES	Elizabeth	3/31/1792
Stephen & Elizabeth OWINGS	Mary Harrowood	2/7/1792
	bapt.	5/6/1792
Samuel & Martha HARPER	Nancy	12/28/1791
James & Priscilla MC COMAS	Cassandra	2/1/1792
George & Mary AMOS	Cassandra	2/23/1792
Robert & Sarah WATT	James	9/25/1791
James & Susanne MONGOMERY	Thomas	2/17/1792
Jacob & Mary GLADDEN	James	4/26/1788
	John	3/26/1790
	Barnet	1/19/1792
Moses & Becky FREELAND	Naomi	1/10/1792
Nicholas & Mary SAMPSON	Thomas	2/3/1792
George & _____ MC CORMACK	Johnson	3/23/1787
John & _____ THOMSON	Lusby	9/24/1787
Alexander & _____ THOMSON	Ann	9/4/1787
James & _____ WARD	James	7/8/1786
John & _____ STREET	Thomas	12/25/1786
Jacob & _____ GLADDEN	Ann	6/5/1787
Robert & Sarah WATT	Sarah	12/10/1786
James & _____ SYNCLEAR	Bailey	10/30/1786
Thomas & _____ WHEELER	Charlotte	5/9/1787
Alexander & Frances CRAWFORD	Margaret	4/16/1777
	George	3/22/1779
	Alexander	2/14/1775
	William	9/11/1786

REGISTER OF BIRTHS & CHRISTENINGS

Parents	Child	Birth Date
William & _____ RUTLEDGE	Benjamin	1/29/1787
Samuel & _____ WADLEY	Hannah	8/24/1787
Samuel & _____ WEBB	Samuel	10/16/1787
John & _____ CARROL	John	5/27/1787
William & Eleanor MARTIN	Alexander	4/25/1785
James & Mary AUSTIN	Hannah	1/14/1787
Alexander & Susanna MC COMAS	Preston	6/7/1787
Mark & Mary MC GOVERN	Mary	9/30/1786
Thomas & Jemima 'STREET	Thomas	11/22/1777
	John	6/26/1779
	Jesse	6/20/1781
	Benjamin	1/18/1785
	Mary	8/4/1787
William & _____ HUTCHINGS	Catharine	10/8/1785
	Susanna	1/31/1787
Joshua & _____ HUTCHINGS	Susanna	4/6/1786
William & _____ KELSOE	Joshua	4/28/1787
_____ & Elizabeth HUTCHINGS	Hannah	3/6/1786
Daniel & Susanna SMITHSON	John Taylor	June 1786
Lyde & Abby GOODWIN	Pleasance	2/12/1780
	Lionel Lyde	11/2/1782
	Charles Ridgely	7/2/1784
	Benjamin	4/12/1786
	Henry	6/18/1787
James & Ann WARD	William	12/19/1787
Nathaniel & Sarah GRAFTON	Martha	5/13/1787
Nathan & Mary SCOTT	Colegate	6/4/1787
Cornelius & Susanna GARRISON	John	3/26/1786
Samuel & Deborah OWINGS	Mary	3/27/1784
	Ann	12/20/1785
	St. Thomas Parrish - BC	
Obadiah & Frances TOWSON	James	1/17/1788
Lemuel (?) & Martha HOWARD	Ann	Aug 1769
Sarah MC CUBBINS	Lloyd	12/11/1782
Joseph & Sarah HART	Sarah	9/3/1781
	Joseph	11/23/1784
	Priscilla	8/26/1788
Abraham & Ruth JOHNSON	Eleanor	4/28/1789
Robert & Temperance LEE	Absalom	9/22/1789
	Caleb	7/25/1788
William & Sarah JOHNSON	William	12/15/1789
William & Eleanor HUTCHINGS	Margaret	11/6/1789
John & Martha CHANCE	Sarah	12/25/1789
Samuel & Elizabeth HICKERSON	Dorcas Baker	9/28/1789
John & Sarah FROST	Joseph	3/17/1790
Joseph & Mary FORD	Mary	10/13/1767
Joseph FORD	bapt. about 49 years old	
Richard & Rachel SAMSON	Ruth	2/21/1789
John & Mary MOORES	James	1789
Barnet & Rachel JOHNSON	Mary	1/7/1790
Robert & Sarah WATT	Elizabeth	3/26/1790

11

Ananias & Cassandra DIVES	Cassandra	8/24/1785
	Sarah	12/10/1787
	Salathiel Galloway	?
Henry & Mary BYFORD	William	1/20/1790
James & Margaret BARTON	John	6/16/1785
	Milly	9/28/1787
Thomas & Ruth ANDERSON	Penelope	11/1/1786
Robert & Jane BRYARLY	Ann	8/14/1789
John & Rachel WHITACRE	Rachel	5/11/1789
	Lauson Mackee	Apr 1781
Thomas & Mary STRAND	Clary	7/26/1789
William ROE	Sarah	1785
	Ann	1787
Thomas & Margaret HOOD	Charles Crook	7/2/1789
Abraham & Elizabeth STANSBURY	Jacob	11/10/1789
David & Heneritta STANSBURY	Daniel	10/19/1788
Ralph & Mary MCCREERY	Letecia	11/10/1788
Richard & Mary COALEY	Mary	10/13/1789
Walter & Sarah BULL	Ruth	3/25/1788
	Walter Billingsly	11/5/1789
Josiah & Rachel SPARKS	Matthew	3/2/1790
Abraham & Hannah COLLET	Aaron	7/31/1789
Joseph & Catheenah BURGES	Joseph	4/20/1790
James & Jane SYNCLEAR	Jane	4/13/1789
Thomas GALLOWAY & wife	Parmela	8/21/1784
	Thomas	11/11/1787
Henry FOSETT	John	11/5/1786
John CORBITT	Robert & Jesse	5/16/1788
Thomas & ____ MILES	Hannah	11/5/1787
Henry & ____ SUTTEN	Elizabeth	10/21/1787
Aquila & ____ MILES	Abraham	8/28/1787
	James	9/24/1787
George & ____ BRIERLY	Ann	5/8/1786
Samuel & Mary JENKINS	Thomas Smith	9/16/1786
Matthew & Prudence SPARKS	Ruth	7/20/1787
Samuel & ____ SHIPLEY	Benjamin	4/25/1788
John Robert & Eleanor Addison HOLLIDAY		
	Prudence Gough	8/1/1785
	Elizabeth Carnan	12/22/1786
	Mary Lee	8/15/1788
	Rebecca Ridgely	?
Joshua & Jemima HUTCHINGS	Salley	9/1/1788
Joshua & Elizabeth SHAW	Nicholas	Oct 1787
John & Catharine DUNNOCK	Thomas	8/25/1787
William & Sarah KEETH	Sarah	2/16/1784
Nathaniel & Hannah SHEPHARD	Mary	5/12/1787
Warral & Noty TRACY	Isaiah	6/22/1788
John & Rebecca TREACY	William	5/8/1785
Moses & Rachel FREELAND	Dorcas	10/9/1787
Samuel & Sarah DOWNS	Henry	5/1/1787
Stephen & Elizabeth AYRS	Rosanna	6/17/1785
Andrew & Elizabeth DILLON	Mary	9/28/1787

REGISTER OF BIRTHS & CHRISTENINGS

Parents	Child	Birth Date
William & Elizabeth SLADE	Matilda	10/16/1783
	Minerva	11/9/1785
	James	7/13/1788
James & Jane DENEATH	Samuel	6/15/1788
_____ & Mary SAMPSON	Elijah	6/6/1788
_____ STERRET	James Riel	12/1/1788
Robert & Martha AMOS	Gabriel	9/30/1788
Asael & Sarah HITCHCOCK	Leah	2/15/1788
William & Mary OLARK	William	1/26/1788
Barnet & Rachel JOHNSON	Thomas	6/6/1788
Charles & Margaret BAYREY	Charles	10/10/1787
	Elizabeth	12/5/1788
James & Martha WEST	Thomas	10/26/1788
Thomas & Ann WEST	Mary	4/15/1774
George & Rebecca BROWN	Elizabeth	10/11/1787
Joseph & Hannah DONAVAN	William	12/15/1788
Thomas & Ann CROMWELL	Henrietta	2/12/1788
Elijah & Elizabeth MERRYMAN	Frances	5/2/1788
Joseph & _____ MC LUNG	Robert	7/26/1787
John & _____ SCOGGINS	Elizabeth	9/17/1787
Jacob & _____ BULL	Jacob	1/23/1786
William & _____ SLADE	Abraham	11/12/1787
James & _____ GOODWIN	Moses	10/12/1787
Dennis & Mary BOND	Harriott	3/17/1788
Nicholas & _____ HUTCHINGS	Menander	9/17/1786
John & _____ SCALF	Barton	11/5/1786
Isaac & _____ AUSTIN	Lawless	7/26/1787
James & Mary ELLIOTT	James	3/10/1788
John & Frances GUYTON	Benjamin	6/3/1788
Joshua & Margaret GUYTON	Sarah	3/7/1788
John & Mary LESOURD	Daniel	7/30/1784
	Peter	6/8/1787
Elijah & Elizabeth STANSBURY	Isaac	6/28/1788
	Jesse	6/29/1786
Henry & Mary ENLOES	Rebecca	8/3/1788
Walter & Belilah TIBITT	Rebecca	8/4/1788
Samuel & Keturah SHIPLEY	Christopher	8/14/1785
	Thomas	12/30/1786
George & Marth SHARP	William	6/21/1787
Adam & Magdalene BURNS	Jacob	9/21/1787
Michael & Mary BURNS	Mary	1/20/1788
Benjamin & Ann PRINE	John	2/11/1787
Frederick & Abilena ALFREED	Susanna	5/1/1786
	Rachel	6/2/1788
Abraham & Ann GUITON	Joseph	3/17/1789
Benjamin & Sarah LEACH	Mary	10/18/1785
	Ann	6/27/1787
Robert & Martha MORGAN	Edward	2/28/1788
Henry & Sarah JONES	Ann	6/3/1789
George & Ann CRUDGINTON	Ann	12/18/1786
Philip & Rachel GRIFFEE	Margaret	1/18/1788
Thomas & Rhoda JOHNSON	Rachel	8/2/1788
Alexander & Priscilla THOMSON	Sarah	4/30/1789

13

Parents	Child	Birth Date
William & Elizabeth HUNT	George	10/12/1788
Abraham & Rebecca RUTLEDGE	Leah	6/17/1785
	Elizabeth	7/8/1787
James & Mary LEEDEN	Ruth	9/2/1788
John & Hannah TURNPAW	Mary	10/28/1788
John & Cloender NIGHT	Christopher &	
	Susanna	12/9/1788
Mesheck & Caranhappock BIDISON	Abraham	3/22/1789
William & Elizabeth GREENFIELD	Mary	5/19/1783
	Elizabeth	2/25/1786
	Sarah	6/11/1788
Esau & Catharine TUCK	John	1/11/1779
	Elizabeth	8/3/1782
	Cassandra	3/1/1784
	James	6/29/1786
	Martha	4/24/1789
Thomas & Ruth ANDERSON	Leonard	4/5/1788
Charles & Deborah GORSUCH	Rachel	9/22/1788
Jesse & Catharine POCOCK	Jemima	1/16/1789
Samuel & Sarah DOWNS	Jesse	4/12/1789
John & Margaret CARR	John	2/27/1784
	Frances	8/5/1786
	Sarah	2/4/1789
Thomas & Rebecca WARE	Benjamin	5/23/1789
Thomas & Rachel SLADE	Micajah	12/24/1788
_____ NASH	Lucresy	9/29/1788
John & Elizabeth RISTEAU	Abraham	5/16/1789
Emanuel & Mary SAMPSON	Margaret	6/22/1789
Thomas & Elizabeth MILES	Lewis	6/24/1789
Isaac & Keziah HOOPER	Michael	7/8/1789
John & Easter HITCHCOCK	Emilia	12/4/1788
Abraham &. B. ENSON	William	10/5/1788
George & Elizabeth LYTLE	George	10/5/1785
	Thomas	2/27/1788
_____ HERINGTON	Elizabeth	12/27/1789
Thomas & _____ MECATHEA (?)	Jehu & Joshua	
	GALLOWAY	5/3/1789
William & Milcah GOODWIN	Achsah	10/3/1775
Abraham & Rachel CORBIN	Nathan	5/3/1788
George & Margaret COLEMAN	Margaret	5/5/1779
Thomas & Sarah MARSH	Charlotte	7/17/1789
Thomas & Ann CROMWELL	Elizabeth Todd	4/30/1790
Joshua & Jemmima HUTCHINGS	Elizabeth	6/11/1790
Thomas & Ruth ANDERSON	Elijah	3/19/1790
Joseph & Mary CURTIS	Sarah	7/18/1787
Benjamin & Mary MERRIMAN	Rebecca	10/24/1787
Abraham & Rebecca RUTLEDGE	Joshua	3/12/1790
Horatio & Catharine BELT	Horatio	7/27/1786
	Thomas Hanson	11/17/1787
	Mary Grafton	9/27/1789
George & Mary FITZHUGH	Grafton Delany	11/7/1787
	Washington	4/1/1789

Parents	Child	Birth Date
Prudence BOSLEY	bapt. 1/1/1790	about 16 yrs old
Jane ENSOR	bapt. 8/1790	25 years
	bapt. 8/1790	8 months
Henry BATEMAN	Lemuel	1/13/1790
John & Mary MCDONNEL	Elizabeth	3/1/1790
Richard & Mary FOWLER	Susanna	12/14/1780
Richard & Mary GAWTHOUP	Asenath	2/4/1790
John & Mary MCDONNEL	Elizabel	3/1/1790
James & Prudence ENLOES	James Marsh	4/20/1790
Benjamin & Sophia HENDEN	Josias	5/25/1790
Charles & Mepheteka ROBINSON	Walter	5/24/1790
	Aquila	7/3/1788
John & Sarah RICHARDSON	James	6/27/1787
	Benjamin	6/21/1790
Simon & Ann NEVILL	Rebecca	2/2/1785
	John	6/26/1787
	Rachel	1/14/1790
Gwin & Delilah WILSON	Lily	5/3/1789
Samuel & ___ WEBB	Percy	Feb 1790
Abraham & Elizabeth HILTON	Nancy	8/1/1790
John & Mary PRIGG	William	2/14/1790
Robert & Elizabeth MCCOLLOUGH	William	June 1783
	Robert	4/10/1786
	Mary	7/10/1787
	Ruth	6/11/1789
John & Ann WEEKS	Mary	6/18/1786
	John	2/8/1788
	Ann	4/10/1789
John WEEKS	bapt.	9/18/1790
	Deer Creek Chapel	
William & Sarah PARMER	Ann	3/26/1790
Samuel & Sarah PARMER	Samuel	6/22/1780
William & Jane SMITH	Nathan	1/22/1781
	Elizabeth	5/23/1785
Samuel & Mary SCARBROUGH	Sarah	7/3/1789
John & Elizabeth CHAMBERLAIN	Samuel	6 yrs &
	all bapt. 9/11/1790	3 mon old
	Philip	4 yrs old
	William	2 yrs old
	Thomas	10 months
Vincent & Sarah WILEY	William	10/20/1785
	John Stephenson	6/5/1789
Joseph & Jimmima WALKER	Richard	3/15/1781
	George	12/14/1782
	Catharine	11/20/1784
	Elizabeth	1/21/1787
Abraham & Rebecca NORRIS	Elizabeth	1/31/1790
Moses & Rachel COLLET	Polley	11/30/1783
	Matilda	11/15/1785
	Jimmima	11/3/1787
	Rachel	9/3/1789

Parents	Child	Birth Date
Asel & Hannah PROSER	Ann	6/7/1785
	David	2/10/1787
	Elizabeth	11/12/1788
	Mary	6/28/1790
Adam & Magdalene BYRNS	Elizabeth	11/20/1789
Isaac & Elizabeth SAMSON	David	5/31/1784
Thomas & Hannah MILLER	John	6/20/1790
Henry & Delea DOWNS	Mary	11/20/1790
Wason & Martha WHEELER	Elizabeth	10/28/1785
	Sarah	1/28/1791
James & Cassandra HAYES	Nicholas	9/12/1788
	George	9/22/1785
	Jesse	8/14/1790
Martin & Mary FUGATE	Edward	7/28/1789
& Ann HAYES	Elizabeth	7/13/1789
John & Cassandra GREEN	Benjamin	9/24/1789
	John	11/12/1790
George & Elizabeth LYTLE	Alexander Mc Comas	5/2/1790
Alexander & Elizabeth STERRETT	William	2/18/1791
William & Elizabeth GORDON	Ruth Gott	5/16/1788
Thomas & Mary BOISE	Thomas	2/11/1790
	Eleanor	8/11/1784
	Rebecca	1/8/1781
	John	3/11/1787
Edward & Eleanor ELIOTT	Samuel	8/12/1790
Thomas & Susanna ELIOTT	Thomas	1/20/1790
John & Elizabeth GREGORY	George Washington	12/14/1790
Robert & Ann JENKINSON	Isabella	3/8/1788
	William	4/1/1785
William & Mary CLARK	Sarah	6/10/1790
James & Ann WARD	Ann Colegate	9/3/1790
John & Jane FLOWERS	Rachel	5/3/1785
	Isabella	10/26/1790
Thomas & Eleanor BARNY	Rhoda	2/15/1791
Thomas & Elizabeth GASH	Michael Ashford	2/10/1790
Charles & Margaret BARY	Bennet	11/27/1789
Arthur & Sarah MONOHON	Arthur	2/11/1791
Joseph & Hannah DONOVAN	Thomas	10/9/1790
Horatio & Catharine BELT	Walter Delany	4/17/1791
George & Mary FITZHUGH	Ann Lee	9/9/1790
John & Lydia HILTON	John	5/3/1791
Obediah & Frances TOWSON	Charlotte	7/21/1790
William & Susanna JAMES	Leah	11/25/1785
	Sarah	7/8/1788
Nathan & Mary LEGE	Nathan	9/3/1790
David & Rachel SHAW	Rebecca	9/12/1790
William & Mary CLARK	Samuel	3/4/1791
& Elizabeth MURREY	Ruth	6/9/1788
Moses & Rachel MAGNESS	Amelia	1/31/1791
William & Rebecca HAMILTON	Elizabeth	7/6/1790
John & Phobe HAMILTON	Phebe Maxwell	3/13/1791
James & Mary SEDDON	George	12/5/1790

16

REGISTER OF BIRTHS & CHRISTENINGS

Parents	Child	Birth Date
Edward & Mary DAY	Juliet	2/14/1790
	bapt. 7/12/1791	
Thomas & Elizabeth GRIFFIN	Martha	4/15/1791
James & Flora STRANGE	son	2/27/1790
Charles & Deley GORSUCH	William	3/8/1791
Nicholas & Elizabeth FULLER	Jemmima	11/30/1787
Abraham & Elizabeth ANDERSON	John	11/2/1788
	Rosannah	8/15/1790
Meshach & Keren-happuch BIDDISON	Salam	3/21/1791
John & Elizabeth WARRICKE	Thomas	10/5/1790
John & Esther HITCHCOCK	Keziah	1/23/1791
Robert & Elizabeth BRYARLY	Ann	9/26/1790
George & Susanna BRYARLY	Thomas	2/28/1791
Christopher & Margaret ANDOEUL (ANDREW?)		
	Rebecca	1/24/1782
	Susanna	5/10/1783
	Joseph	10/3/1785
Nathaniel & Rebecca PHIPPS	John	6/ 7/1791
John & Mary MOORES	Samuel Lee	12/5/1790
Parker Hall & Elizabeth LEE	Blanch Hall	2/25/1791
James & Ann MCCOMAS	Amos	8/13/1785
	Sarah	12/28/1787
	Clemency	10/12/1790
John & Ann WEEKS	Sarah	8/21/1791
Robert MC CULLOCK	Benjamin	6/9/1791
Henry & Sarah JOHNS	Henry Hosier	4/3/1791
Edward & Sarah COWIN	Rosanna	8/7/1787
	Hugh	9/12/1789
William & Mary SCARBROUGH	Arsbel	5/20/1791
James & Alkee KEY	John McDaniel	5/1/1791
Jesse & Mary FOSTER	Faithful	10/31/1790
Alexander & Cassandra CROOKS	Ann	6/30/1791
Samuel & Mary SCARBROUGH	John	3/20/1791
	James	8/10/1786
Thomas & Mary STROUD	Ann	8/15/1791
Francis & Ann BARNHOUSE	John	5/4/1791
Andrew & Catharine TAYLOR	Elizabeth	10/17/1788
Samuel & Mary MORGAN	Edward	2/7/1774
William & Susanna PRIGG	Edward	10/18/1791
Isaac & Susanna HITCHCOCK	Israel	6/24/1791
Asael & Sarah HITCHCOCK	Abraham	3/10/1790
Patrick & Sabrai TODD	Elizabeth	10/11/1789
James & Margaret RIGLEY	Margaret	2/15/1785
William & Eleaner JORDON	Ann	7/2/1786
	Sarah	7/16/1788
	Eleaner	6/2/1790
Josiah & Charity HITCHCOCK	Aquila Clark	11/30/1787
	Ann	5/1/1791
James & Martha NEWALL	Elizabeth Claypole	Dec 1790
William & Dorothea DIMMET	Jacob	7/12/1791
John & Mary MCCOMAS	Sarah	1/21/1787
	Elizabeth	7/25/1790

17

REGISTER OF BIRTHS & CHRISTENINGS

Parents	Child	Birth Date
Henry Leonard & Cathrenah Mary MILLER		
	John Joseph	6/15/1787
	John Martin	12/27/1788
Nicholas & Deborah MERRYMAN	Eleaner	8/16/1790
Dennis & Mary BOND	Jane	10/25/1789
Joshua & Ann HATRARTY	Abraham	6/20/1792
Robert & Mary CRAITON	Letitia Richardson	1/13/1792
Thomas & Elizabeth AIRS	Joshua	5/13/1790
Matthew & Margaret COWLEY	Eleanor	5/4/1791
Richard & Sarah SHORES	Sarah	8/9/1786
	John	7/26/1788
	Margaret	12/19/1790
George & Elizabeth NORRIS	Edward	9/15/1791
Jeremiah & Sarah AIRS	Sarah	10/6/1791
Adam & Magdalene BURN	Sarah	Dec 1791
William & Elizabeth MOOBERY	Jane	10/8/1789
	Ann	8/21/1791
Lancelot & Ann CARLILE	Lancelot	Nov 1789
	James	Feb 1792
John & Elizabeth TAYLOR	James	12/11/1789
	Corban	8/27/1791
Samuel & Mary HUTCHINGS	Thomas	5/24/1784
	Elizabeth	4/26/1786
	Sarah	5/15/1790
	Two blacks William & Sy TOOGOOD	
James & Mary ASHTON	James	5/11/1790
William & Ann ISGRIGG	Robert	12/1/1791
Samuel & Belinda WEBB	Isaac	6/2/1791
Henry & Sarah MYERS	George	1/19/1792
John & Sarah MERRYMAN	Catharine	2/14/1792
William & Elizabeth STEWARD	Henry Guyton	5/26/1791
Thomas & Rachel SLADE	Isaac Whidiker	4/25/1792
John & Mary PHIPPS	William	11/15/1782
	Mary	4/30/1785
	John	7/24/1787
Robert & Mary RENSHAW	Elizabeth	3/3/1786
	Ann	9/15/1788
	Catharine	7/3/1791
James & Ann POCOCK	Sarah	6/6/1787
	Daniel	4/1/1789
	James	7/27/1791
____ & Mary FOSSET	Margaret	3/31/1792
Nicholas & Ann HUTCHINGS	Joshua	12/5/1791
Thomas & Penelope KELSO	Elijah Rutledge	11/18/1791
William & Elizabeth PORDUE	Laban	7/12/1791
George & Kizziah ELLIOTT	Abraham	1/22/1792
John & Margaret SCOGINGS	William	7/17/1792
Barnet & Sarah BOND	Josias & William twins	Winter 1792
	bapt.	9/7/1792

18

Parents	Child	Birth Date
_____ & Mary MATTOCKS	Charity	1792
	bapt.	10/7/1792
John & Frances GUYTON	Eleanor	5/9/1792
	bapt.	10/14/1792
Samuel & Nancy CRAG	Samuel	3/17/1789
	William	Nov 1792
	bapt.	10/18/1792
		[sic]
William & Elizabeth HARVEY	James	1792
	bapt.	10/18/1792
	Ruth, a Negro child	same day
Abraham & Elisabeth STANSBURY	Ruth Edwards	5/1/1792
John & Mary MCGOWAN	Catharine Johnson	6/23/1792
_____ & Sarah WOOD	Achsah	11/17/1792
Lyde & Abba GOODWIN	Maria	9/11/1792
	bapt.	Oct 1793
William & Dorcas CLARK	Sophia	7/29/1791
	bapt.	11/5/1792
William & Mary LIDDON	George	8/10/1792
	bapt.	11/5/1792
Leonard & _____ COSEY	Letty	3/19/1792
	bapt.	11/5/1792
Lawrence & _____ LYNCH	Mary	11/11/1787
	Eleanor	3/23/1789
	Frances	9/30/1790
	Eliza	5/18/1792
Joseph & Elisabeth BROWNLEY	Thomas Archer	4/20/1781
	Catharine	11/29/1783
	James Stewart	11/30/1786
	John Smith	7/2/1789
Joseph BROWNLEY	bapt.	Aug 1789
E. F. BROWNLEY	bapt.	Aug 1789
Edward & Elisabeth FLANAGAN	William Sligh	4/1/1779
	Sophia	1/7/1786
	Maria	6/8/1789
James AMOSS of Mordecai &	Benjamin	10/26/1789
Susanna AMOSS	William	9/30/1792
Aquila & Mary GREER	James	2/6/1790
	William	12/31/1791
Robert & Martha AMOSS	Elizabeth	2/3/1790
John & Cordelia BULL	Elizabeth	8/3/1785
	John	11/3/1786
	William	3/11/1788
	Richard	2/9/1790
	all baptized	8/5/1792
Flemmon & Eleanor KELL	Francis	7/16/1790
Nathan & Sarah CORBAN	Abraham	3/15/1789
	bapt.	8/26/1792
Joshua & Jemmima HUTCHINGS	Richard	2/25/1792
Martin & Mary FUGATE	Forest	9/17/1792
	bapt.	11/11/1792
Henry & Mary SUTTON	William	8/19/1792
	bapt.	11/17/1792

Parents	Child	Birth Date
Henry & Hannah RUMSEY	Maria	7/7/1790
	bapt. soon after birth	
	Amelia Jane	4/14/1792
	bapt.	11/18/1792
Esau & Catharine LUCK	Mary	June 1791
Edward & Sarah FLINCHAM	Mary	11/17/1791
	bapt.	12/9/1792
John & Mary MOORES	Aquila Paca	10/27/1792
	bapt.	12/11/1792
John & Elizabeth SEWEL	Bazzel	2/26/1792
	bapt.	12/17/1792
Caleb & Sarah COCKEY	Lewis	4/17/1791
	Sarah	10/14/1792
	1 Negro Henry bap.	12/24/1792
Robert & Temprance LAY	Penelope D.	5/15/1792
_____ & Mary HOLDER	Priscalla	3 yrs old
Thomas & Catharine COOPER	Mary	7/15/1779
	Sarah	12/2/1780
	Hester	7/29/1782
	Ann	6/10/1785
	Elizabeth	4/28/1787
	John Gorsuch	6/6/1790
	Eleanor	9/7/1792
	all baptized	1/24/1793
John & Mary DEMOSS	Aquila	5/19/1790
	Jimmima	10/25/1792
	Both baptized	2/3/1793
Benjamin & _____ HENDON	Joshua	1789
Arranias & Cassandra DIVERS	Priscilla Galloway &	
	Elisabeth	1/25/1793
Augustine & Elizabeth BAYLES	Martha D.	12/6/1790
	Nimrod	12/10/1792
	Both baptized	3/10/1793
Joshua & Augustine RUTLEDGE	Elizabeth	1793
John & Margaret IRWIN	Effee	10/13/1790
	Anna	8/7/1792
Francis & Margaret DICKENS	Hannah	8/28/1791
Edward & _____ COYIN	Elisabeth	2/21/1792
Benjamin & _____ SEDGWICK	Benjamin	1/31/1793
Rastes & Susanna CALGAL	Henry	2/14/1785
	Daniel	5/11/1788
William & Jane _____	Thomas	5/12/1792
James & Catharine HULET	Matthew	8/17/1792
	bapt.	3/30/1793
John & Ann GRIFFIN	Rebecca	12/2/1792
Hercules & Elisabeth STONE	Eleanor	Feb 1790
Elisabeth MCLEES		1/20/1779
	bapt.	4/4/1793
Nathan & Mary SCOTT	Ruth	1/18/1793
	bapt.	4/6/1793
Richard & Mary GAWTHROUP	Thomas	11/24/1792
Jonathan & Mary COLE	Elisabeth	11/27/1792
	bapt.	4/7/1793

Parents	Child	Birth Date
John & Elisabeth JACKSON	Sarah	2/12/1792
James & Mary WEBSTER	Susanna	10/24/1787
	Mary	9/18/1789
Isaac & Kizziah HOOPER	Asael Wilson	12/2/1791
	bapt.	4/14/1793
Leonard & Catharine METTEE	Leonard	5/5/1792
Aaron & Elisabeth GORDON	Rebecca	14 mo old
		in May 1792
Samuel & Susanna' RICKETTS	Hannah Rebecca	2/2/1793
John & Mary MCGAW	Richard	12/16/1792
Gittings & Jane WILSON	Jane	3/26/1791
Thomas & ____ KELSO	Jane	2/25/1790
	bapt.	5/12/1793
Richard & Elisabeth GRAY	Elisabeth	4/24/1793
John & Mary GERMAN	Thomas	about Sep 1792
James & Frances HUGHES	James	3/28/1793
William & Viney REED	Aaron Tunis	1/21/1792
Daniel & Elisabeth REES	Mary	5/24/1793
	bapt.	6/2/1793
George & Kizziah CUNNINGHAM	Mary	8/26/1792
Edward & Mary DAY	Ishmael	3/20/1792
	bapt.	6/16/1793
William Fell & Latitia DAY	Pamella	1/1/1791
	Cassandra Fulton	5/28/1793
Abraham & Elisabeth HILTON	Patty	1/13/1793
John & Nancy FOWLER	Reuben	4/30/1792
Henry & Catharine FLETCHER	Zachariah	2/25/1793
	bapt.	6/30/1793
Arthur & Margaret ELLIOTT	John Taylor	2/18/1788
William & Rachel ELLIOTT	Ann	10/27/1790
Michael & Mary BURN	Jacob	8/27/1791
Thomas & Mary RICHARDSON	Benjamin	1/13/1792
Fridrick & Abololey ELSWOOD	John Frederick	1/30/1793
Jacob & Catharine SPLETSTONE	Adam	2/16/1793
Alexander & Martha _____	James	3/26/1792
John & M. BAXTER	Isabella	4/28/1771
	Mary	11/10/1791
Asael & Susanna BARTON	Nancy Wilson	7/7/1790
	William Wilson	6/18/1792
	Margaret Wodden	3/4/1793
	bapt.	7/14/1793
John & Lydia FLETCHER	William	5/3/1785
	James	Dec 1787
	John	8/3/1788
	Elisabeth	4/1/1792
Samuel & Elisabeth FULLER	John	7/1/1793
Samuel & Ann FRANCIS	Sarah	8/23/1790
James & Eleanor FELL	Polly	5/29/1793
William & Rachel HOGGES	John	7/8/1785
	William	7/30/1788
	Allen	Aug 1789
	Samuel	3/25/1792

21

REGISTER OF BIRTHS & CHRISTENINGS

Parents	Child	Birth Date
Samuel & Ann FRANCIS	Charles	5/12/1780
	William	10/2/1782
John & Elisabeth POTTER	Cordelia	6/6/1792
Lovlis & Elisabeth GORSUCH	William	4/30/1793
Charles & Ruth CANOLE	Ruth	6/9/1793
James & Rebecca RICHARDSON	Eleanor	4/10/1786
William & Susanna JAMES	William	8/22/1791
Henry & Mary MARTIN	Samuel	1793
Thomas & Sarah COWLEY	Milcah	10/20/1792
Benjamin & Taratius ROBERTS	Mary	4/5/1792
William & Bothier BISHOP	Elijah	10/20/1780
	Esther	9/20/1786
	Jemima	10/6/1788
	Rebecca	11/1/1792
John & Lydia HILTON	Abraham	6/11/1793
	bapt. on or about	7/28/1793
Josias & Rachel SPARKS	Aaron	5/17/1787
	Francis	5/11/1792
	bapt.	8/4/1793
William & Margaret MCFADDEN	Ann	5/11/1792
	bapt.	8/11/1793
Thomas & Leah HARTLEY	Mary	9/9/1792
	Ezekiel	1792
	bapt.	Sep 1793
Barnet & Rachel JOHNSON	Sarah	1791
Elisha & Catharine BOWEN	Benjamin	3/23/1789
	Josias	7/28/1793
John & Margaret HARWOOD	Walter	3/26/1793
Walter & Sarah BULL	Sarah	8/5/1791
	Walter	8/2/1793
	bapt.	9/28/1793
Solomon & Dinah DIZNEY	Nancy	8/31/1793
Esau & Catharine LUCK (TURK?)	George	9/15/1793
David & Priss (Negroes)	Fanny	Mar 1793
James & Mary SUDDEN	Aquila	8/15/1793
George & Sarah ELLENDER	Nicky Grimes	4/20/1793
John & Elisabeth GRIMES	Polley	11/17/1792
Moses & Rebecca FREELAND	Ann	7/17/1793
Abraham & Mary FREELAND	Elisabeth	7/8/1792
John & Alice LIGHTFOOT	Elisabeth	7/19/1793
Joshua & Athaliah ROE	Edward	9/15/1790
	Isham	8/12/1792
Samuel & Rebecca MORRIS	Belinda	4/14/1792
Jonathan & Susanna PLOWMAN	Jonathan	12/13/1792
Michael & Elisabeth RUTLEDGE	Penelope	10/8/1792
Thomas & Elisabeth AYRES	James	6/7/1793
John & Catharine DUNNUCK	Rachel	6/24/1793
Benjamin & Sarah LEACH	Nephel	7/24/1791
	Elisabeth	6/4/1793
John & Elisabeth TWYBLE	David	10/4/1792
William & Mary HART	Mary	4/11/1792
	bapt.	10/12/1793
Walter & Mary BOSLEY	Charles	2/17/1793

22

Parents	Child	Birth Date
William & Elisabeth CHINWORTH	Susanna	7/9/1791
Thomas & Sarah MARSH	Rachel	8/20/1791
	Sophia	9/21/1793
	bapt.	10/22/1793
William & Elisabeth HUNT	Ruth	9/2/1792
James & Elisabeth MCCOMAS	Mary	8/17/1782
	Josias	11/30/1785
Thomas & Penelope	Ann	6/14/1793
John & Sarah MERRYMAN	Elisabeth Johnson	10/11/1793
Hugh & Mary WILEY	Ann	10/22/1789
	Loby, Black child	1/15/1792
William & Susanna PRIGG	William	3/18/1793
John & Polley MCCUBBINS	Zaccariah	10/18/1792
Polley MCCUBBINS	bapt.	23 yrs old
	both bapt	1/19/1794
Moses & Elisabeth MCCOMAS	Josiah Scott	7/5/1782
	bapt.	1/21/1794
Stephen & Lucy OWINGS	William	3/28/1788
	Elisabeth	12/30/1789
	Nicholas	7/9/1791
	all bapt.	1/25/1794
John & Elisabeth JACKSON	Elisabeth	9/3/1793
	bapt.	2/13/1794
Samuel & Martha HARPER	Elisabeth	9/29/1793
	John	2/6/1791
	bapt.	2/15/1794
Thomas & Rachel AYRES	Mary	1/6/1793
	bapt.	2/15/1794
James & Ann MCCOMAS	James Preston	3/22/1792
	bapt.	2/15/1794
William & Priscilla SLADE	James Whittaker	7/25/1793
	bapt.	2/15/1794
David & Hannah STREET	Isabella	12/28/1793
	bapt.	2/15/1794
James & Priscilla MCCOMAS	Elisabeth	7/21/1793
	bapt.	2/15/1794
Peter & Margaret LONG	Nancey	7/14/1792
	bapt.	2/15/1794
Temperance JENKINS	Henry	10/14/1793
	bapt.	2/15/1794
James & Sarah SMITH	Franklin James	Feb 1786
	Sarah	10/12/1784
	bapt.	3/25/1794
John & Sarah EATON	David	11/30/1786
	Joseph	5/1/1788
	Samuel	2/9/1790
	Alee	10/15/1791
	John	1/17/1794
Gavin & Delilah WILSON	Bethia	3/1/1794
	bapt.	4/14/1794
John & Ann FOWLER	Harriot	1/8/1794
Mesick & Kirenhappuck BIDDISON	Daniel	11/26/1793

23

Parents	Child	Birth Date
Aquila & Ann HALL	William Henry	11/11/1793
	bapt.	5/22/1794
Alexander & Martha GARRETT	Rosanna	3/2/1794
	bapt.	5/25/1794
David & Hannah STREET	Thomas	5/1/1794
James & Susanna MONTGOMERY	Abraham	11/24/1793
William & Elisabeth MCCLURE	Sarah	1/10/1794
John & Charity HEAPE	Mary	4/2/1792
	Sarah	12/24/1793
Robert & Sarah WATT	Nancey	5/2/1794
Thomas & Jemmima STREET	Sarah	12/10/1794
Elijah & Elisabeth STANSBURY	Jacob	6/17/1793
Nathan & Magdalene BRINLEY	Nathaniel	2/3/1794
Jesse & Rachel KENT	Nancy	5/12/1780
Mordecai & Hannah AMOS	Hannah	7/30/1791
	Thomas	4/27/1794
	Vincent	8/23/1788
	Mordecai	3/18/1790
John & Martha STREET	Sinclair	2/1/1788
	Charlotte	2/4/1794
	bapt.	6/2/1794
William & Rachel ELLIOTT	Sarah	9/29/1793
Josias & Rebecca BULL	Anna	7/25/1793
John & Mary MILLER	James	8/10/1792
Adam & Magdalene BURN	Stephen	11/5/1793
John & Hannah HERRINGTON	Sarah	2/27/1792
	Betsey	9/1/1793
	both bapt.	5/2/1794
Henry & Deley DOWNS	Samuel	2/11/1794
	bapt.	5/5/1794
James & Grace FIFE	John	5/2/1792
	bapt.	5/5/1794
Henry & Alce HOWARD	Grace	11/1/1793
	bapt.	5/5/1794
John & Sarah MILLER	Samuel	1/27/1794
	bapt.	5/5/1794
Ananias & Cassandra DIVERS	Ann	Feb 1794
	bapt.	4/13/1794
John & _____ DAY	Young	
	bapt.	6/8/1794
John & Elisabeth WARRICK	Jenney	10/13/1792
	bapt.	7/27/1794
Aquila & _____ MILES	Caty	1/2/1794
John Taylor & Hannah HUGHES	Elisabeth	10/5/1790
	Taylor	8/24/1792
Michael & Elisabeth GILBERT	Elisabeth	12/7/1791
	bapt.	10/19/1793
John & Sarah COOLEY	Charlotte	2/29/1791
	bapt.	10/19/1793
Robert & Elisabeth MORGAN	Elisabeth Hawkins	3/11/1793
	bapt.	10/19/1793

Parents	Child	Birth Date
Henry & Rachel BOWMAN	Benjamin	5/2/1791
	John	8/16/1793
	bapt.	10/19/1793
Henry & Sarah MILLER	Edward	5/15/1791
	Jacob	5/31/1793
	both bapt.	10/19/1793
William & Elisabeth MOOBERY	William	11/18/1793
Henry & Margaret BRYARLY	Isabella	7/10/1790
Robert & Elisabeth BRYARLY	Elisabeth	9/29/1793
William & Margaret RUTLEDGE	Mary	4/17/1791
	Shadrack	5/27/1792
	Belinda	9/2/1793
	Sarah	4/18/1794
Robert & Sarah BRYARLY	Jonathan Lyon	1/18/1793
	Anne	1/7/1787
	both bapt.	7/26/1794
John & Hannah SCARF	John	12/16/1786
	Mary Fullerton	5/16/1793
James & Penelope KIDD	Joshua Hardesty	12/14/1791
	Rhoda	4/13/1794
James & Elisabeth SHEREDINE	Elisabeth	1/27/1792
Isaac & Jane MCNABB	Sarah	9/25/1793
	bapt.	8/17/1794
Thomas & Rachel SHARP	Horatio	All 3
	James Eliott	born
	Betsey Ann	7/6/1794
Nathaniel & Hannah SHEPHARD	Elisabeth	4/10/1794
William & Ann CURTIS	Rachel	2/2/1794
Thomas & Cassandra KELLEY	William	1/10/1794
	bapt.	8/10/1794
Jonathan & Elisabeth PAUL	Susannah	9/14/1786
James & Mary LOGAN	Alexander	3/4/1785
	Joseph	3/13/1787
	Jane	7/22/1782
John & Sarah WADSWORTH	Thomas Dunkin	4/16/1794
	bapt.	Sep 1794
Michael & Elisabeth GILBERT	Elisabeth	12/7/1795
John & Sarah COLEY	Charlotte	2/29/1791
Robert & Elizabeth MORGAN	Elizabeth Hawkins	3/11/1793
Henry & Rachel BOWMAN	Benjamin	5/2/1791
	John	8/16/1793
Henry & Sarah MILLER	Edward	5/15/1791
	Jacob Colson	5/31/1793

On September 10, 1794 at Synclair's funeral 8 or 10 children were baptized, their names not entered.

Vincent & Sarah WYLE	Thomas Sutton	8/31/1793
	bapt.	11/30/1794
Barnet & Jane JOHNSON	David	4/15/1794
Thomas & Ann JOHNSON	John	4/23/1794
William & Mary CLARK	Ruth	3/25/1793
	bapt.	12/10/1794

Parents	Child		Birth Date
James & Susanna MURRY	Mary		7/9/1794
Shadrack & Rachel GREEN	Matilda		6/23/1792
	bapt.		12/30/1794
Abraham & Elisabeth HILTON	John		10/13/1794
	bapt.		2/20/1795
William & Sarah JARMAN	Rachel		10/11/1794
	bapt.		2/20/1795
John & Elisabeth POTTER	Thomas		6/5/1791
	bapt.		2/20/1795
Thomas & Sarah BOND	Tobias	about	10 yrs old
	Alice	"	8 yrs old
	Joshua	"	6 yrs old
	Mary	"	18 mos old
	all bapt.		3/30/1795
Abraham & Elisabeth STANSBURY	Ruth James Edward		9/20/1794
Joshua & Jemima HUTCHINS	Frances		10/26/1794
Nathan & Mary SCOTT	Benjamin Colegate		2/23/1795
	bapt.		5/4/1795
John & _____ MONKS	William		1/2/1787
	Anna Bella		9/12/1789
	Louisa		3/1/1793
	Mary Ann		2/12/1791
	Elicia		1/25/1795
Dr. Jacob & Mary HALL	Mary		10/10/1793
Benjamin & Mary NICHOLSON	Eleanor		10/24/1786
	Benjamin		8/17/1788
	Sarah		4/7/1790
John & Elisabeth JACKSON	John		5/25/1795
	Juliet		2/12/1792
	bapt.		4/19/1795
William & _____ OSBURN	Harry Page		4/1/1794
Absalom & Rebecca GALLOWAY	Methia		?/26/1790
	Elisabeth		10/23/1790
	bapt.		5/20/1795
Joshua & Jane MILES	Margaret	about	2 yrs old
	Rebecca	"	7 mos old
	both bapt.		6/11/1795
James & Penelope KELSO	John	about	12 mos old
	bapt.		6/11/1795
Samuel & _____ WEBB	Elisabeth	about	12 mos old
	bapt.		6/11/1795
John & _____ LEACH	Mary	about	10 mos old
	bapt.		6/11/1795
William & _____ GROVER	Charles	about	11 mos old
	bapt.		6/11/1795
Nathan & _____ FITZPATRICK	Priscilla	about	4 mos old
	bapt.		6/11/1795
James & Sarah WITHERAL	William		5/6/1795
George & Nancey CLARK	Daniel		9/29/1794
	bapt		6/21/1795
George & Kizziah CUNNINGHAM	George		2/13/1795
Arthur & Ann BARNLEY	John		5/14/1795
Benjamin & Amelia CARROLL	Sarah		2/1/1795

26

Parents	Child	Birth Date
James & Ann NORRIS	Hannah	9/13/1794
	bapt.	6/21/?
Henry & _____ MYERS	Henrietta	9/7/1795
Jacob & Mary GLADEN	Jacob	7/15/1794
William & Hannah GLADEN	Jane	12/24/1793
Matthew & Margaret COWLEY	Abraham	10/30/1794
James & Elisabeth BURK	Margaret	3/26/1795
_____ & Eleanor STANSBURY	Mary Slade	12/2/1793
_____ & Mary NORRIS	John	11/4/1793
James & Ann EVERITT	William	10/23/1794
Richard & Lydia STANDIFORD	Elisabeth	12/21/1794
	bapt.	6/28/?
_____ & Rebecca YARDLEY	Mehala	7/5/1785
	Ralph	12/25/1788
	both bapt.	7/5/1795
Abraham & Methia ENSOR	Mary	4/12/1790
William & Charity HALL	Elisabeth Ann	7/26/1793
Norman & Keturah GORSUCH	Nicholas Norman	4/9/1795
Edmond & Mary SAWYER	Mary	5/15/1792
	William	7/13/1794
George & Patty WRIGHT	Rachel	10/14/1787
	bapt.	7/11/1795
George & Elisabeth LYTLE	Nathan	9/4/1792
	bapt.	7/12/1795
John & Mary DEMOSS	Susanna	6/22/1795
	Elijah Rutledge	3/20/1795
Charles & Eleanor ROCKHOLD	Elijah	5/20/1795
Josias & Rebecca Ball SLADE	Lucy Smith	12/7/1794
Joshua & Margaret GUYTON	Martha	4/17/1795
	Eleanor	12/22/1792
Jeremiah & Ann CULLAM	John Wilks Howland	5/21/1790
	Margaret	5/20/1793
	Harriott	8/20/1795
John & Martha CHANCE	Frances	8/24/1792
	Wealthian	11/27/1794
John & Sarah GUYTON	James	July 1795
John & Cassandra GREEN	Mary Ann	1/16/1793
	Thomas Smithson	2/20/1794
Dorcas BUCK	bapt.	6/20/1795
Asael & Susanna BARTON	Ann	12/15/1794
James & Susanna MONTGOMERY	James	9/6/1795
Jacob & Mary GLADDEN	Frederick	7/25/1795
Peter & Margaret LONG	James	7/6/1794
James & Susanna AMOS	Elisabeth	12/17/1794
Mordecai & Rachel AMOS	James	8/20/1795
James & Priscilla MCCOMAS	Scott	12/4/1794
David & Mary POCOCK	Sarah	10/3/1795
Joseph & Constant BURTON	Delia	8/1/1791
	Pleasance	11/14/1795
	bapt.	12/24/1795
James & Elisabeth GIVEN	Rachel	12/9/1795
Jacob & Achsah STOVER	Elisabeth	Jan 1796

Parents	Child	Birth Date
Thomas & Ann WRIGHT	Harry about 2 1/2 yrs old	
	? " 3 mos old	
	bapt.	4/30/1796
Robert & Elisabeth PEAK	Robert	8/14/1795
Edward & Elisabeth FLANNAGAN	John Holliday	7/28/1792
	Achsah Holliday	7/28/1792
John & Catharine ALLEN	James	1/31/1796
	bapt.	4/24/1796
Ananias & Cassandra DIVERS	Mary Galloway	5/28/1795
Derumple & Elisabeth ASKEW	Betsey	1/18/1795
	bapt. at Joppa	
	St. Johns	5/8/1796
Isaac & Martha STRAWBRIDGE	Barbara	1/5/1796
	Nell's Sall	1/5/1796
George & Fanny BROWN	?	5/15/1796
William & Elisabeth ONION	Rebecca Weston	1796
Jesse & Catharine POCOCK	Ann	3/15/1794
	Eli	3/29/1796
William & Ann CURTIS	John Shephard	5/28/1795
Francis & Mary HARE	John	10/18/1795
Wason & Sarah WHEELER	Wason	8/15/1795
John & Margaret SCOGINGS	Penelope	8/13/1795
Walter & Elisabeth PERDUE	Mary	3/2/1795
Thomas & Elisabeth TALBOTT	Belinda	11/22/1795
Aquila & ____ MILES	Joshua	4/9/1796
William & ____ HUTCHINGS	Joshua	1/23/1796
Elihu & Hannah DAVIES	Charles	?
John & Ann PARKER	Isham	3/28/1796
Samuel & Penelope FRAZER	Mary	3/14/1793
	William	11/3/1794
David & Hannah STREET	Glenn	7/12/1795
Christopher & Kizia BUCK	Benjamin	12/18/1795
Joseph & Ruth GRIFFIN	Lynch	3/25/1796
Aquila & Elisabeth PARK	William	8/16/1795
George & Sarah COLLINS	Caty Maria	3/19/1796
Abraham & Elisabeth HILTON	Betsey	6/18/1796
John & Elisabeth GREGORY	Elisabeth	10/13/1795
Charles & Fiduky	Aley	7/9/1794
Gwin & Delilah WILSON	Charlotte	8/10/1796
George & Sarah ELLENDER	Joshua	4/26/1795
Philip & Rachel GRIFFIN	James	1/29/1796
	bapt. between May 15th & Sept.	
		29, 1796
William & Dorcas INGLE	William	1795
Joshua & Ellenor BIVEN	James	Aug 1787
James & Mary SILK	Nancy	7/25/1791
	John	11/24/1793
	James	8/8/1796
Thomas & ____ SYNCLEAR	James	1794
at Coop Town	bapt.	10/4/1796
Thomas & Elisabeth SADLER	Mary Ann	9/28/1794
	Frances	3/21/1796
William & Elisabeth HUGHES	William Plummer	2/22/1794

28

Parents	Child	Birth Date
Aquila & Ann HALL	Aquila	5/27/1795
Thomas Gassaway & _____ HOWARD	Frances Cordelia	11/13/1795
	Eliza August	10/22/1791
William & _____ ALLENDER	John Wane	5/5/1796
	bapt.	9/25/1796
Jeremiah & Eleanor JOHNSON	Elisha Sollers	2/10/1791
Hickman & Ann JOHNSON	George William	2/14/1794
	Elisabeth Sollers	9/24/1795
	bapt.	11/18/1796
Nicholas & S. HUTCHINGS	Sarah	5/28/1796
	bapt.	12/1796
Robert & Rebecca BALLARD	William about 13 yrs old	
	bapt.	2/3/1797
John & Elisabeth GUYTON	James	10/28/1796
Thomas & Mary HEAPE	Isabella	7/3/1796
Henry & Sarah MYERS	Sarah	2/17/1797
Thomas & Temperance AMOS	Scott	9/29/1796
John & Charity HEAPE	Jesse	12/18/1796
William & Sarah DAWSON	Isaac	3/2/1786
Samuel & Martha HARPER	Harriot	12/4/1795
	bapt.	4/20/1797
Thomas & Ann JOHNSON	Barnet	1/23/1796
Barnet & Jane JOHNSON	James	1/31/1796
Robert & Sarah BRYARLY	Mary Ann	12/25/1796
George & Elisabeth DAVIES	William	10/4/1796
	bapt.	4/6/1797
Francis & Sarah DINES	William	1/22/1787
	Lovy	3/30/1789
	Elisabeth	6/22/1791
	John	5/31/1795
William & Ann ISGRIGG	Thomas	10/5/1796
Thomas & Catharine LAMBDAN	George	1/29/1794
	John	12/25/1796
	bapt.	4/19/1797
Isaac & Elisabeth BOSLEY	Mary	1/24/1796
David & Mary POCOCK	Robert	2/12/1797
	bapt.	4/30/1797
James & Martha DULY	Salley	1/18/1797
	bapt.	5/2/1797
William & Elizabeth MOOBURY	Alexander	7/23/1796
		York Co., Pa.
James & Ann COLLINS	John	7/14/1795
	Nathan, a Negro child 9 mos	
	bapt. at the Manor Chh 5/14/97	
Joseph & Agness REED	Mary	4/11/1797
Moses & Rachel COLLET	John	8/5/1791
	Susanna	5/16/1794
	Moses	7/3/1796
Leonard & Cathrine METTEE	Henry	12/5/1796
Christopher & Elisabeth BULL	John	7/5/1796

29

Parents	Child	Birth Date
William & Mary WHEELER	Sarah	3/1/1786
	Kitty	1/6/1788
	George	11/19/1789
	Ruth	12/26/1790
	Mary	4/13/1796
George & Margaret PARMER	Eleanor	9/17/1796
Thomas & Hannah MILLER	Robert	2/12/1797
John & Jemima _____	Achsah	10/14/1790
	John	1/6/1797
Wason & Sarah WHEELER	Anna	1/6/1797
	bapt.	5/29/1797
Leonard & Mary COURSEY	Mary	6/1796
John & Ann FOWLER	Ruth	3/17/1797
Thomas & Elizabeth JACKSON	William	11/24/1796
	bapt.	6/7/1797
Richard & Mary FOWLER	James	9/12/1796
William & Mary CLARK	Barnet	10/23/1795
Elisha & Catharine BOEN (BORN?)	Robert	4/26/1795
	Rebecca	2/10/1797
John & Margaret HOWARD	Elisabeth	3/19/1795
	bapt.	5/13/1797
	George	6/6/1796
Samuel & Ann FORWOOD	Sarah	10/3/1796
David & Hannah STREET	Abraham	11/12/1796
Elisha & Catharine BOWEN	John	2/26/1789
	William	11/27/1791
Francis & Nancy BARNHOUSE	Thomas	3/8/1797
	bapt.	6/24/1797
Nicholas & Deborah MERRYMAN	Nicholas	6/20/1793
William & Marget MARKEY	Rebecca	11/22/1796
	bapt.	6/25/1797
Walter & Catharine DALLAS	Catharine Reed	8/26/1796
Solomon & Rachel DISNEY	William	1/23/1797
David & Rachel GUISHARD	Sarah	5/29/1796
John & Ann WILSON	Mary	11/14/1793
	Joseph	5/15/1795
Robert & Elisabeth PEAK	James W.	4/29/1792
	Catharine	1/11/1794
	John	6/13/1797
James & Margaret BARTON	Thomas Smithson	3/18/1790
	Mary	1/18/1793
	Ann	3/18/1795
	Elisabeth	7/21/1797
Richard & Sarah HARRITT	Jane	3/10/1792
	Sarah	1/5/1796
	Henry	3/11/1797
William & Mary NORRIS	John Philips	8/22/1796
Walter & Elisabeth PERDEW	William	3/19/1797
Benjamin & Alice _____	Abraham	2/19/1797
Fredrick & Nancy MOPS	Fredrick	Feb 1796
Richard & _____ WATE	Diana	9/29/1792
	Richard	1793

Parents	Child	Birth Date
Lovelace & Elisabeth GORSUCH	Nathan	3/20/1795
	Jesse	2/10/1797
Charles & Eleanor ROCKHOLD	Jesse	5/17/1797
	bapt. between 8/30 &	9/4/1797
Walter & Sarah BULL	Pamelia	12/8/1796
Dickinson & Mary GORSUCH	Elisabeth	4/2/1797
	bapt.	9/17/1797
William & Sarah JONES	Archibald	7/31/1796
	Thomas Johnson	Feb 1786
_____ & Frances JAMES	Elisabeth	2/11/1794
	Ann	2/13/1797
Aquila & Alice ARMSTRONG	Sarah	5/14/1797
	bapt.	10/29/1797
Larkin & Rachel SMITH	James Baxter	7/29/1797
	bapt.	10/29/1797
James & Mary SHEREDINE	Ruth	8/31/1797
	bapt.	11/2/1797
James & Elisabeth COOPER	Rachel	11/25/1797
Benjamin & Rachel GARMAIN	Job	6/30/1797
John & Catharine BUCK	Benjamin Merryman	6/18/1797
Aquila & Ann HALL	Edward Carvill	11/13/1797
	bapt.	12/2/1797
John & Elisabeth JACKSON	Harriott	6/7/1798
Thomas & Ann WRIGHT	Joshua	2/3/1798
Robert & Susanna PORTER	James	1/2/1798
	bapt.	3/1798
William & Ann GALLOWAY	Priscilla	8/14/1797
	bapt.	3/1798
Christopher & Kezia BUCK	Joshua	1/30/1798
	bapt.	3/1798
William & Mary ANDREW	Priscilla	9/11/1797
	bapt.	3/1798
Thomas & Eleanor BARTON	Mary	8/17/1797
	bapt.	3/1798
Above baptized 3/1798 were baptized at Benjamin Buck's.		
Joseph & Elisabeth Ann GRINDALL	Eliza Helen?	3/10/1798
Meshack & Kirenhappuck BIDDISON	Shadrack	11/17/1795
	Ann	3/11/1798
Leonard & Mary COEN	Elisabeth	3/12/1798
George & Nancy CLARK	Mariah	3/23/1797
John & Lydia HILTON	Kitura	12/27/1797
	bapt.	3/10/1798
Vincent & Penelope RICHARDSON	Skelton Standiford	7/11/1797
Jesse & Mary HITCHCOCK	Sarah	8/13/1796
	bapt.	5/26/1798
Henry & Hannah RUMSEY	Charles Henry	8/14/1796
Barnet (of Barnet) & Jane JOHNSON	Robert	10/18/1797
Thomas & Ann JOHNSON	Margaret	12/22/1797
William & Mary CLARK	Hester	3/26/1798
	bapt.	6/8/1798
Edward & Clary BRADLEY	Susanna	11/31/1789
	Mary	11/9/1791

Parents	Child	Birth Date
John & Mary Magdalene KEETH	Ann Hart	2/5/1796
	Mary Magdalene	10/23/1797
John & Sarah MERRYMAN	Levi	12/1795
	Ann Mariah	12/17/1797
John, Jr. & Sarah DUNNUCK	Joseph Sutton	12/22/1797
Thomas & Elisabeth AYRES	Samuel	4/19/1798
	Susanna	2/7/1796
William & Cordelia ANDERSON	Abraham G.	3/11/1798
Joshua & Mary ANDERSON	Juliet Elisabeth	12/2/1793
John & Catharine DUNNUCK	Catharine	11/25/1796
_____ BRADLEY	Hannah Rutledge	10/13/1795
	Sarah	7/24/1797
Dixon & Elisabeth SLADE	Washington	2/27/1795
	Edward	4/3/1796
	Matilda	4/21/1798
John & Elisabeth TWIBLE	Martha	6/3/1795
	bapt.	6/24/1798
Stephen & Elisabeth SPLITSTONE	William Montgomery	4/27/1798
Abraham & Elisabeth ANDERSON	Ira	8/1/1792
	Jemmima	12/15/1794
	Cordelia	8/19/1797
	bapt.	6/24/1798
Abraham & Elisabeth HILTON	William	4/13/1798
Thomas & Elizabeth JOHNSON	Elisha	9/17/1797
Joshua & Margaret GUYTON	Margaret	6/16/1798
Arthur & Sarah MONOHON	Charlotte	8/27/1792
	James	1/11/1798
	Blanch	11/5/1798
William & _____ MCFADDIN	William	1/1/1794
	Charles	9/22/1795
	Thomas Wilson	2/27/1798
Thomas & Anne SHEREDINE	John	6/8/1798
Elijah & Ann SPARKS	Ann	10/21/1798
Thomas & Ruth ANDERSON	Ann	10/5/1798
David & Sarah JOHNSON	David	9/21/1786
	Sarah	3/24/1789
	Thomas	1/29/1791
	Benjamin	1/24/1793
	Mary	6/10/1795
Charles & Delia GORSUCH	Karunhappuck	1/2/1795
	Charles	2/27/1798
Thomas & Jemima HUTCHINGS	Susanna	9/24/1791
	John	3/31/1796
William & Eleanor HUTCHINGS	Edward	6/5/1798
James & Elisabeth BRADY	Ruth	5/22/1798
George & Sary ELLENDER	Elisabeth	7/9/1798
	6 Black children	
John & Elisabeth HOCKLEY	Elisabeth	8/12/1798
Gaum & Delilah WILSON	Edward	2/26/1798
John & Mary HOWLAND	Ann	2/22/1798
Benjamin & Terrecen (?) ROBERTS	Zachariah	9/13/1796

REGISTER OF BIRTHS & CHRISTENINGS

Parents	Child	Birth Date
Zachariah & Susanna AMOS	Sarah	11/27/1793
	Levi	9/12/1795
	Philip	3/18/1798
John & Naomi CALDER	Sophia	3/30/1798
David & Hannah STREET	Mary	1/5/1798
Aquila & Martha MCCOMAS	Robert Amos	2/28/1798
Robert & Elisabeth AMOS	Martha	5/20/1792
	Sarah	2/20/1794
	Benjamin	5/6/1796
	Mary Ann	5/20/1798
Josias Slade & Rebecca BULL	Betsey Ann	12/4/1796
	Rebecca	3/20/1798
_____ & Elizabeth LONG	Aquila	11/6/1790
Daniel & Sarah AMOS	John Johnson	12/5/1793
	Robert Clark	9/25/1795
	Ann	1/28/1798
John & Elisabeth LYTTLE	John	9/30/1798
	bapt.	3/31/1799
		St. Johns
Darby & Mary LUX	Elisabeth Ann	11/26/1798
	bapt.	4/6/1799
		St. James
Thomas & _____ AYRES	Elisabeth	3/9/1798
	bapt.	4/13/1799
		St. James
Eliakim & Parmelia JAMES	William	10/6/1798
St. Johns Parish	bapt.	5/14/1799
Walter & Delilah TIBBITT	Elisabeth	8/18/1791
St. James Parish	Joshua	12/28/1798
	bapt.	7/7/1799
Charles & Sally ELDER	Violetta Elisabeth	4/22/1799
St. Thomas Parish	bapt.	8/5/1799
Joshua & Sarah BUCK	James	11/17/1793
St. Johns Parish	Sarah	3/3/1798
John & Elisabeth GREGORY	John N. Grimes	3/30/1798
St. Johns Parish	bapt.	8/20/1799
Michael & Catherine MASON	George	5/16/1799
	Ann	8/27/1797
John & Rachel LEAFE	Rebecca	1/27/1798
John & Rebecca BAILEY	Thomas	7/7/1798
Thomas & Elisabeth RITTER	Sidney	12/1/1798
Jacob & Elisabeth HOOK	Sarah	11/20/1798
St. Thomas Parish	bapt.	9/1/1799
John Ensor & Mary STANSBURY	Ruth Edwards	9/15/1797
William & Susanna HYOT	William	1/15/1794
Abraham & Elisabeth STANSBURY	James Edwards	2/26/1799
St. Johns Parish	bapt.	9/23/1799
Adam & Mary BURNS	John	10/22/1797
Joseph & Agnes READ	Hugh	6/5/1799
Joshua & Jemima HUTCHINGS	Ann	12/17/1796
	Ariel	4/20/1799
Patrick & Elisabeth LYNCH	William	2/20/1799
Jacob & Mary SCHREADER	Elisabeth Johnson	8/21/1797

33

Parents	Child	Birth Date
Benjamin & Rachel STANDIFORD	William	2/28/1798
William & Elisabeth SLADE	Levi	4/9/1798
James & Ann POCOCK	Ann	9/4/1798
Abraham & Elisabeth SAMPSON	Abraham	11/15/1798
William & Mary TYSON	William	4/16/1798
Dickinson & Mary GORSUCH	Belinda	5/25/1799
Jesse & Catharine POCOCK	Charity	4/22/1798
Stephen & Elisabeth SPLITSTONE	Rebecca	8/5/1799
William & Ann CURTIS	Thomas	1/20/1799
Abraham & Ann BRUSBANKS	William	9/20/1797
	Mary	8/21/1799
Michael & Mary BURNS	Sarah	2/26/1799
	Rachel	7/10/1797
Frederick & Apalona ELSROOT	Michael Gall	11/9/1798
Samuel & Belinda WEBB	Margaret	7/31/1797
Josias & Catharine SLADE	Thomas	6/17/1796
Aquila & Elisabeth MILES	Elisha	6/25/1798
George & Hannah GRAYHAM	Catharine	9/2/1795
	Sarah	2/2/1797
	Elisabeth	7/1/1799
Francis & Mary HAIR	Susanna	5/8/1799
_____ & Sarah ROCKHOLD	Thomas	7/3/1799
	bapt.	10/6/1799
	St. James	
William & Ruth MACKEY	James Howard	6/12/1799
	bapt. St. Thomas	11/4/1799
Joshua & _____ GIST	Federal Anna Buoneparte	-----
	bapt.	11/4/1799
Samuel & Ruth OWINGS	William Lynch	8/7/1799
St. Thomas	bapt.	11/17/1799
George Chocke & Elisabeth NORRIS	Mary	11/7/1797
St. James	bapt.	11/7/1799
William & Elisabeth MOOBERRY	David	10/7/1798
of York City, state of Penna.	bapt. St. James	11/13/1799
James & Harriett GITTINGS	John Sterrett	5/22/1798
St. Johns Parish, BC (or St.James?)	bapt.	11/15/1799
John & Elisabeth MERRYMAN	Eleanor Cassandra	12/29/1799
Leonard & Catharine METTEE	John Jacob	9/23/1799
Moses & Rachel COLLET	Ann	9/6/1798
Nicholas & Sarah MERRYMAN	Mary	6/11/1799
St. James	bapt.	1/29/1800
John Barry & Harriet DARLEY	Elisabeth	1/22/1800
St. Thomas Parish	bapt.	2/2/1800
Robert & Sarah BRYARLY	Deliverance	12/8/1798
Barnet & Jane JOHNSON	Ann	10/6/1799
David & Hannah STREET	Sarah Lorrinsa	5/12/1799
Thomas G. MORFORD	Thomas Garrison	6/17/1738
St. Thomas Parish	bapt.	4/6/1800
David & Mary POCOCK	Daniel Smith	12/15/1799
William & Sarah FULLER	Nancy	1/11/1800
David & Sarah JOHNSON	Ellenor	9/29/1799
St. James Parish	bapt.	4/10/1800
Rogers & Catharine STREET	Thomas Corben	8/4/1799

Parents	Child	Birth Date
John & Elisabeth GLADDEN	Sarah	9/21/1798
Thomas & Ann JOHNSON	James	9/18/1799
St. James Parish	bapt.	4/30/1800
Beal & Ruth OWINGS	Eliza	8/25/1798
Abraham & Margaret FONDY	Mary	8/15/1799
Joshua & Mary BROWN	Joshua	6/15/1799
Fredrick & Mary HARP (HASP?)	James	9/18/1799
Michael & Rebecca GLADMAN	Ann	2/2/1798
Daniel & Susanna CARR	Elisabeth Ann	11/25/1799
Elias & Ann BROWN	Prudence Ann	4/21/1799
St. Thomas Parish (Chapel)	bapt.	5/25/1800
Francis & Mary LONDERSLAGER	Jacob	12/28/1798
St. Thomas Parish	Elisabeth	6/23/1800
	bapt.	9/28/1800
Peter & Mary SHOCK	William	6/2/1799
George & Margaret BALMER	Margaret	3/18/1799
Samuel & Sarah HUGHES	Elisabeth	9/18/1799
William & Ann WHEELER	William	2/7/1798
	Ann	1/20/1800
Adam & Susanna ROSER	Joseph & Elisabeth	11/5/1799
	(twyns)	
Daniel & Prudence WALKER	Mary	11/20/1799
St. James Parish	bapt.	6/18/1800
Charles & Elisabeth JONES	Elisabeth Robinson	2/28/1800
St.Thomas	bapt.	6/29/1800
Thomas & Mary SUTTON	Benjamin	2/19/1800
William & Elisabeth SLADE	Penelope	4/20/1800
Charles & ____ JOHNSON	Edward	4/6/1800
Isaac & Elisabeth BOSLEY	Elisabeth	12/10/1797
Aquila & Elisabeth MILES	Margaret	4/17/1800
Claudius & Susanna HITCHCOCK	Elisabeth	4/5/1800
Josiah & Rebecca BULL	Balinda	8/6/1799
Thomas & Elisabeth TALBOTT	Mary	1/5/1800
Michael & Mary BURNS	Susanna	2/26/1800
St. James	6 Blacks bapt.	8/3/1800
Larkin & Rachel SMITH	Eleanor Larmming	6/19/1799
	bapt.	8/7/1800
St. James Parish	3 Blacks bapt. at same time	
Jesse & Mary HITCHCOCK	Susanna Garland	9/19/1798
St. Thomas Parish	bapt.	8/24/1800
Jacob & Sarah GLADDEN	William	1/29/1797
William & Hannah GLADIN	William	2/7/1796
	Mary	5/19/1798
Henry & Sarah AYRES	Henry	3/14/1798
John & Catharine FOSTER	Aaron	12/16/1799
John & Ann RANGE	Sarah	3/27/1800
John & Charity HEAP	Ann Kent	2/16/1798
	Elisabeth	3/22/1800
Thomas & Mary HEAP	William Bankhead	5/25/1800
St. James Parish	bapt.	8/27/1800
Archibald & Elisabeth GITTINGS	Ann	6/15/1800
St. James Parish	bapt.	8/28/1800

REGISTER OF BIRTHS & CHRISTENINGS

Parents	Child	Birth Date
Rogers & Catharine STREET	Glenn	7/25/1800
St. James	bapt.	8/27/1800
Jesse & Catharine POCOCK	Eleanor	4/22/1800
James & Lydia WADSWORTH	Thomas	12/26/1798
John & Nancy NORRIS	Thomas	2/24/1800
Joshua & Charlotte RYAN	John Mead	10/17/1799
St. James	Zaccariah of Nathan & Mary	
	CHALK, a Black child	
	bapt.	10/20/1800
St. James Parish	bapt.	10/20/1800
Benjamin & Ann SMITHSON	Martha Howard	1/22/1796
on their way to Virginia	bapt.	11/4/1800
St. Thomas Parish		
Abraham & Sarah HICKS	Rebecca	8/29/1800
Robert & Ann DUN	James	2/22/1799
Wann & Sarah WHEELER	Delilah	2/25/1800
	Temperance	5/11/1798
James & Pensely KIDD	Letitia	1/24/1798
	James	5/15/1800
Richard & Mary HILL	Lewis	3/6/1796
	Elisabeth	8/5/1798
	William	1/1/1800
John & Mary CARLTON	William	12/6/1794
St. James Parish	bapt.	11/11-12/1800
Edward & Susan DORSEY	Patience L.	4/23/1788
St. Thomas Parish	Leven L.	12/19/1799
Living in AC	bapt.	12/16/1800
Stephen & Ann WHEELER	Joseph Stansbury	9/23/1800
Nicholas & Sarah MERRYMAN	Benjamin	7/16/1800
Samuel & Martha HARPER	Joshua	9/27/1797
	Clemency	9/19/1799
Robert & Sarah WATT	David	2/11/1795
	William	11/9/1798
Thomas & Jemima STREET	Elisabeth	6/15/1789
bapt. St. James Parish	Rachel	4/13/1791
Nov. 22, 24 & 25th	Sarah	12/10/1793
	Samuel	11/15/1800
Solomon & Anne LONDERSLAGER	Cecelia	9/26/1800
St. Thomas	bapt.	11/30/1800
Thomas & Christiana RAMPLEY	Mary	10/7/1800
St. James	bapt.	12/26/1800
Bryan & Elisabeth PHILPOT	?	
Hickman & Ann JOHNSON	Eleanor Caroline	5/26/1798
	bapt.	2/13/1801
	Henrietta HOOD - a free yellow	
	child abt. 2 yrs old bapt at	
	old Mr. Johnson's same day,	
		2/13/1801
George & Sary HEALTY	James	10/12/1798
	John	12/10/1800

36

Parents	Child	Birth Date
John Talbot & Elisabeth RISTEAU	William McLaughlin	2/18/1791
St. Thomas Parish	Thomas Cradock	12/21/1795
	Robert Carnan	3/2/1799
	Charles Walker	7/14/1797
	Benjamin Denny	11/24/1800
	bapt.	2/17/1801
Thomas & Mary RINGGOLD	John Galloway	10/20/1800
St. James Parish	bapt.	3/21/1801
Joshua & Margaret GUYTON	Josiah	11/6/1800
Ralph & Jane BOND	Elisabeth	11/5/1789
St. James Parish	bapt.	4/5/1801
Thomas & Mary RICHARDSON	Jamima	Sep 1799
Edmond & Hannah STANDIFORD	Isaac	5/12/1800
Abednigo & Mary TOWSON	Joshua	4/18/1795
	Elisabeth	4/22/1800
Margaret BOYLES	Deliah	6/13/1794
Joshua & Augustine RUTLEDGE	Nancy	11/2/1800
St. James Parish	bapt.	May 1801
John Norris SHOCK	bapt.	9/25/1800
Martha WILSON	bapt.	2/2/1800
Robert & Sarah BRYARLY	Elisabeth	3/7/1801
Thomas & Sarah STREET	Maria	3/11/1801
Eliakim & Parmelia JAMES	Juliana	2/6/1801
John & Nancy CALDER	Matilda	2/24/1801
Zachariah & Susanna AMOS	Elisabeth Baldwin	12/13/1799
Widow TAYSON	Elisabeth	6 yrs old
	Elijah	3 yrs old
	Mary & Cassandra twins 1yr old this day	6/8/1801
John & Mary DEMOSS	Ruth	3/13/1801
Thomas & Mary ST. CLAIR	Mary Ann	4/5/1801
Josias Slade & Rebecca BULL	Josias Slade	1/19/1801
David & Hannah STREET	David	11/25/1800
James & Susanna MONTGOMERY	Nancy	7/26/1797
John & Mary CHARLTON	John	2/3/1787
	Catharine	4/3/1789
Thomas & Rachel AYRES	Matilda	6/8/1801
St. James Parish	bapt.	6/1801
Thomas & Elisabeth PIERCE	John Bacon	12/19/1800
St. James Parish	bapt.	7/5/1801
Jacob & Ruth WAGGONER	Barbary	10/28/1800
St. Thomas Parish	bapt.	6/29/1801
Jacob & Mary SCHREADER	Jacob D.S.	6/6/1800
George & Eleanor RIGBY	George	4/8/1801
John & Jane HAMBLETON	James	7/13/1799
	William	5/1/1801
Loveless & Elisabeth GORSUCH	James	12/14/1799
St. James	Rachel	1/28/1801
	bapt.	8/7/1801
Andrew & Ann BUCHANAN	Dorothea	12/30/1800
St. Thomas	bapt.	8/6/1801

37

REGISTER OF BIRTHS & CHRISTENINGS

Parents	Child	Birth Date
Nicholas Ruxton & Sarah MOORE	Rebecca	10/23/1794
St. Thomas or St. Pauls	Gay	5/16/1801
	bapt.	8/31/1801
John & Elisabeth VAUGHAN	Rachel	11/30/1800
George & Elisabeth NORRIS	Daniel Tredaway	10/27/1793
	Esrom Hughes	9/21/1795
Joseph & Letice BOSLEY	Nicholas	5/21/1801
Stephen & Elisabeth SPLITSTONE	Jacob	11/25/1800
Adam & Mary BURNS	William Bull	12/26/1800
Isaac & Elisabeth BOSLEY	Letice	12/21/1800
Robert & Elisabeth BARTON	Mary	5/16/1801
Joseph & Mary CURTIS	Levi	9/8/1800
Samuel & Sarah HUGHES	Ann Bull	4/1/1801
George & Margaret PARMER	Edward	3/5/1801
George & Elisabeth NORRIS	Greenberry Wiley	1/30/1800
St. James Parish	bapt.	9/4/1801
Fredrick & Apalinia ELSROODS	Dorcas	3/8/1801
Walter & Elisabeth PERDEW	Walter	6/18/1801
Joshua & Elesiana SHAW	Elisabeth	12/22/1800
James & Ann POCOCK	Rachel Fugate	5/8/1801
James & Cassandra HAYES	Ann	12/19/1793
Jesse & Catharine POCOCK	Kezia	5/29/1801
John & Elisabeth PRICE	Joseph	9/18/1801
Elijah & Elisabeth SAMPSON	Elijah	9/9/1799
John & Ann ALMONY	Benjamin	1/1/1799
	James	7/10/1801
William & Ruth AMOS	Julianna	5/5/1801
Thomas & Elisabeth AYRES	Thomas	4/15/1801
William & Mary TYSON	Richard	3/4/1800
Henry & Mary SUTTON	Ruth	10/9/1795
	Ann	9/9/1798
John & Sarah DUNNUCK	Luk Wiley	11/26/1799
John & Jemima DUNNUCK	Sarah	8/2/1801
St. James Parish		
John & Frances GUYTON	Jesse	5/18/1801
St. Johns Parish	bapt.	9/28/1801
John GUYTON		
Samuel & Arrianna OWINGS	Julianna	8/19/1795
St. Thomas Parish	Rachel	9/6/1799
	bapt.	11/26/1801
Thomas & Sarah WODSWORTH	Jannet	11/26/1793
St. James Parish	Mary Ann	2/14/1796
	bapt.	11/30/1801
William & Ann CURTIS	Levi	10/23/1801
St. James		
Samuel & Rachel HUGHES	Joshua	10/15/1801
St. James Parish	bapt.	12/27/?
Thomas & Catharine FORD	Catharine	10/18/1798
St. Thomas	bapt.	12/8/1801
James & Sarah WINCHESTER	Samuel	11/5/1800
Richard & Mary CROMWELL	Elisabeth	1/23/1801
St. Thomas	bapt.	1/24/1802

38

Parents	Child	Birth Date
Abraham & Sarah ANDERSON	Sarah	8/28/1799
St. James	Ann	9/10/1801
	bapt.	1/5/1802
Bryan & Elisabeth PHILPOT	John	10/1801
St. Thomas	bapt.	2/9/1802
William & _____ RICHARDSON	William Altee	4/17/1801
St. Thomas		
Barnet & Jane JOHNSON	Barnet	4/13/1801
John & Elisabeth JACKSON	James	9/6/1799
	Edward	8/2/1801
Samuel & Ann CRAGE	Lovey	1/15/1802
William & Mary CLARK	Ann	11/3/1800
Robert & Sarah WATT	John	9/22/1801
St. George Parish	bapt.	6/8/1802
Archibald B. & Elisabeth GITTING	Elijah Bosley	3/6/1802
St. James	bapt.	5/31/1802
Robert & Sarah CRAWFORD	Ann	4/9/1800
St. Thomas Parish	bapt.	6/21/1802
William & Sarah FULLER	Elisabeth	10/27/1801
John & Hannah FULLER	John Hutchings	4/15/1802
Dickinson & Mary GORSUCH	Thomas Talbott	11/1/1802
St. James Parish		
Lancelott & Ann CARLISLE	Larkin	4/6/1797
	bapt.	7/26/1802
Aquila & _____ MILES	John	1/29/1802
William & Elisabeth MOOBERRY	John	2/2/1801
York City, Pennsylvania	bapt. St. James	9/2/1802
Stephen & Mary CROMWELL	Richard Arthur	12/2/1801
St. Thomas	bapt.	6/6/1802
John & Ann BEATY	Mary	11/4/1799
	William	7/11/1802
Josiah & Mary BLEANY	Melissey	2/15/1802
Thomas & Mary SUTTON	Joseph	4/22/1802
St. James	bapt.	Sep 1802
James & Sarah SMITH	Daniel	2/28/1802
Benjamin & Selinah SEDGWICK	Rachel	6/25/1802
Joshua & Mary FLEAHARTY	Sarah	3/6/1802
_____ & Priscilla JONES	Mary	2/9/1790
Charles & Mary JONES	Stephen	6/3/1798
	Mary	9/19/1801
William & Rebecca BEVARD	Rebecca	4/16/1802
David & Mary FLOWERS	James	12/9/1801
_____ & Elisabeth FATE	Margaret	3/18/1802
St. Georges Parish	bapt.	11/1/1802
William & Hannah GLADDEN	Elisabeth	3/30/1805
Robert & Sarah WATT	Anna	2/1/1804
Edward & Susanna LEE	Anna	3/20/1804
Thomas & Eleanor JORDAN	Mary	8/14/1805
John & Hannah ADAMS	Elisabeth	10/11/1802
	Sarah	2/25/1805
George & Jamimi BOND	Elisha	5/30/1805
David & Hannah STREET	Edward Rigby	11/7/1795
	Hannah	7/10/1805

Parents	Child	Birth Date
Thomas & Ann JOHNSON	Robert	5/24/1805
Nicholas & Sarah MERRYMAN	Martha	4/9/1802
	Ann	7/21/1805
	bapt.	1805
William & Mary TYSON	Rachel	12/12/1802
George & Elisabeth NORRIS	George	3/6/1802
James & Elisabeth KELSO	William	6/29/1802
Ephraim & Susanna RUTLEDGE	Elisabeth	8/5/1802
St. James	bapt.	9/26 & 27/1802
Thomas & Elisabeth JOHNSON	Mary Ann	10/4/1802
St. Johns	bapt.	11/25/1802
John L. & Elisabeth RISTEAU	Richard Casson	8/30/1802
St. Thomas	bapt.	2/18/1803
William & Mary WETHERALL	George Henry	6/16/1802
St. James	bapt.	2/1803
Aquila & Alice ARMSTRONG	Elisabeth	1/28/1802
Josias S. & Rebecca BULL	John	12/30/1802
Benjamin & Alice ELLIOTT	Benjamin	11/3/1802
St. James	Ruth Gott	8/14/1789
____ & Elisabeth PEARCE	William	7/25/1802
Roger & Catharine STREET	Jefferson	9/25/1803
David & Hannah STREET	Robert	5/26/1802
John & Mary PARMER	John Ellis	11/20/1802
Joseph & Jane WARD	John	9/2/1802
William & Hannah GLADDEN	Jacob	10/21/1799
Samuel & Nancy CRAIGG	Margaret	2/17/1801
Francis & Ann BARNHOUSE	William	7/14/1798
St. James or St. Georges near	Nancy	12/1/1802
Deer Creek		
Robert & Sarah BRYARLY	Hannah	11/20/1802
St. James	bapt.	4/24/1803
James & Hannah BOSLEY	Elisabeth	11/12/1802
Jesse & Catharine POCOCK	Israrel	10/1/1802
St. James		
John & Elisabeth SINGLETON	Martha	7/20/1793
St. George's	Thomas	3/24/1795
	John	9/1/1796
	Nancy	8/28/1798
	William	2/7/1800
	Phebe	11/9/1801
	bapt.	11/27/1802
Thomas & Mary SUTTON	Nicholas	6/13/1803
Manor St. James	bapt.	7/31/1803
Thomas & Mary GITTINGS	Eleanor Croxall	12/18/1802
St. Thomas	bapt.	7/27/1803
James & Lydia WADSWORTH	James	1/20/1802
Peter & Martha BASHAM	Matilda	1/27/1800
Dixon & Elisabeth SLADE	Elisabeth	4/15/1802
Thomas & Jamima TURNER	Aquila	1/20/1802
John & Rachel MAGNESS	James	10/2/1802
Andrew & Sarah WILEY	Joseph	10/11/1796
St. James	Joshua Cooper	3/11/1803
Thomas & Mary SPARKS	Rachel	4/24/1803

REGISTER OF BIRTHS & CHRISTENINGS

Parents	Child	Birth Date
William & Ann RAMPLEY	Elisabeth	5/28/1803
John & Ann ALMONY	Elisabeth	4/18/1803
Elijah & Elisabeth SAMPSON	Anna	1/1/1803
Thomas & Catharine WILLIAMS	Joshua	5/7/1802
St. James		
Clement & ____ MARSH	Thomas Beale	12/15/1799
St. James	James Elliott	7/25/1801
	bapt.	9/17/1803
Jacob & Achsah STOVER	Jacob	1797
St. Thomas	Sophia	1799
	Susanna	1801
Matthew & Jane STACY	Catharine	9/17/1802
St. Thomas	bapt.	10/9/1803
Charles & Elisabeth JONES	John	7/21/1801
	Charles	4/6/1803
William & Mary CLARK	Merrim	7/17/1802
St. Thomas	bapt.	9/4/1802
Thomas & Christiana RAMPLEY	Patty Mayes	1/20/1792
	Phillemon	2/1/1801
	Susanna Mayes	4/6/1801
	William	1/11/1803
	Charles Mayes	4/14/1803
	James	8/11/1803
	bapt.	9/4/1803
James & Ann STARR	Ann	7/18/1800
St. Thomas	Sarah	5/30/1803
Nicholas (of Benj.) & Sary MERRYMAN		
St. James	Gerard	12/24/1803
	bapt.	1/29/1804
Isaac & Elisabeth HAYES	Harriot	12/26/1802
Luke & Sarah WEST	Gassaway	4/12/1792
St. Johns	bapt.	4/18/1804
Robert & Martha GROVER	Martha Prigg	6/9/1803
St. George	bapt.	4/19/1804
Joshua & Margaret GUYTON	Elisabeth	4/26/1803
Henry & Sarah MILLER	Jesse	9/22/1803
Matthew & Mary KENARD	Howard	8/25/1803
William & Ann CURTIS	Sarah	9/16/1803
St. James		
Samuel & Rachel HUGHES	Vincent	1/7/1804
John & Elizabeth LITTLE	William	1/31/1804
Luke & Charlotte WYLE	Thomas	3/22/1804
Abraham & Rachel VAUGHAN	Elizabeth	10/7/1803
St. James	bapt.	May & June 1804
Charles G. Ridgely & Ruth INGRAM	Charles Edward	7/10/1804
St. Johns	Ridgely	
	bapt.	9/3/1804
David & Mary POCOCK	Mary Ann	5/4/1804
Robert & Sarah BRYARLY	Appiah	3/18/1804
John & Elisabeth JACKSON	Martha	2/12/1804
Aquila & Alice ARMSTRONG	Solomon	6/1/1804
William CLARK, Jr. & Mary	Barnet Johnson	1/28/1803
Thomas (of Barnet) & Ann JOHNSON	Thomas	7/20/1803

REGISTER OF BIRTHS & CHRISTENINGS

Parents	Child	Birth Date
James & Eleanor MCCLUNG	Mary Ann	aged 2 years
St. George & St. James		& 6 mo
	bapt.	12/8/1804
Robert & Mary WILLIAMS	Eleanor	6/24/1802
	Ann Yellott	8/23/1804
Nancy STANDIFORD	Luther Thomas	7/15/1804
St. Johns	bapt.	12/26/1804
Peter & Betsey HUNTER	William	5/22/1797
Benjamin & Rachel VAUGHAN	Rebecca Gott	3/23/1802
St. James		
?	Joshua K. FULLER	4/15/1804
Thomas & Elisabeth DULEY	Charlotte	4/22/1804
Edward & Jemima MORRIS	Electius	9/3/1803
Edward MORRIS		
Titus & Priscilla HOLLINSHADE	John Smith	10/1/1803
Ephraim & Susanna RUTLEDGE	Mary	9/5/1804
Frederick & Appelona AILSROD	Bilinda	8/13/1802
Henry & Comfort WINE	Mary Ann	9/19/1803
James & Nancy COOPER	Mary	5/11/1804
Samuel & Sarah HUGHES	Jemimah	Dec 1803
Michael & Mary BURNS	Catharine	Dec 1802
William & Mary TYSON	George	3/22/1804
Rice & Christana WILLIAMS	Sarah	6/6/1804
James & Hannah BOSLEY	Nancey	2/28/1804
Hickman & Ann JOHNSON	Hithe Hickman	5/7/1803
Bryan & Elisabeth PHILPOT	Elisabeth Hance	8/10/1804
Stephen & Mary CROMWELL	Elisabeth Ann	8/5/1804
St. Thomas	bapt.	1/8/1805
Thomas & Rachel ELLIOTT	Catharine	12/20/1803
St. James	bapt.	1/10/1805
Ignatius & Kerenhappuck OHARROW	Sally	12/28/1803
St. James	bapt.	1/10/1805
Francis & Ann BARNHARROW	Mary	3/1804
John & Ann NORRIS	James	2/23/1804
Thomas & Mary SUTTON	Thomas	12/9/1804
John & Sarah DUNNUCK	Hellen	2/1/1805
John & Elisabeth PRICE	John	1/20/1805
William & Sarah CURRIN	Edward Fugate	12/15/1804
Rogers & Catharine STREET	Aberilla	12/22/1804
Joseph & Jane WARD	William	6/27/1804
Wasten & Sarah WHEELER	Ariel	2/20/1805
Peter & Martha BAHEN	Elisabeth	2/1/1805
William & Mary HART	William	10/12/1805
Elijah & Elisabeth SAMPSON	Rachel	9/9/1805
	bapt.	1805
Henry R. & Mary AMOS	John Street	2/23/1804
Joseph & Agness REED	Agness	12/30/1804
John & Sarah RICHARDSON	John	3/8/1792
	Sarah	3/3/1794
	Jamima	5/21/1797
	David	12/25/1798
	Mary	10/21/1802
	Samuel	7/28/1804

42

REGISTER OF BIRTHS & CHRISTENINGS

Parents	Child	Birth Date
Thomas & Catharine LAMBDEN	Kitty	8/30/1801
	Elijah	1/24/1804
	bapt.	1805
John & Sarah MILLER	Bethia	6/6/1805
John & Susanna ASHTON	Joseph	9/6/1801
St. Johns	Hannah	11/23/1802
	John	11/21/1804
	bapt.	1805
William & Frances STANSBURY	Samuel	June 1804
St. James	Maria & Lewis 2 Yellow	
	children bapt.	8/25/1805
Thomas G. & Martha S. HOWARD	Susanna	3/12/1804
Charles & Eleanor ROCKHOLD	Ann Eleanor	8/29/1803
St. James		
John & Mary CAIERNS (KERNS?)	James	11/7/1805
St. James		
Joseph & Ruth SHEETS	Thomas Owings	6/1/1803
	Ruth Caroline	11/22/1804
Basil & Susanna SOLLERS	Ruth	5/29/1802
St. Thomas	Susanna	5/31/1804
Leonard & Jermima ELLIOTT	Kezia	9/8/1805
Benjamin & Alice ELLIOTT	Mary	9/27/1805
St. James	bapt.	4/3/1806
Thomas & Sarah SPARKS	Rachel	4/24/1803
Loveless & Elizabeth GORSUCH	Nicholas	9/22/1802
	Eleanor	6/20/1805
Dickinson & Mary GORSUCH	Dickinson	9/22/1805
John & Elisabeth SLADE	Sally Ann	9/14/1805
St. James	bapt.	6/29/1806
Joshua & Jemima HUTCHINGS	Ellenider	1/1/1801
	Nicholas	6/17/1805
William & Hannah NELSON	Sarah	10/2/1805
William & Ellinder HUTCHINGS	Ellen Maria	2/20/1806
Jesse & Jemima HUTCHINGS	John	10/24/1805
St. James	bapt.	7/13/1806
John & Rebecca PRESTON	Chloe Ady	9/16/1805
John & Elisabeth JACKSON	Anna Maria	2/4/1806
Christ's Church Harford Co.		
William (?) & Elisabeth SLADE	Mary	1/27/1802
Jesse & Catharine POCOCK	Mary	2/9/1806
William & Elisabeth MOOBERRY	Samuel	12/17/1804
living in York County Town-		
ship, Pennsylvania	bapt. St. James	
Luke & Charlotte WYLE	Joshua	11/2/1805
Josias & Comfort ANDERSON	Rachel	1/14/1805
Samuel & Rachel HUGHES	Luther	2/5/1806
Joseph & Letty BOSLEY	Mary	6/12/1805
St. James		
Robert & Mary WILLIAMS	Hannah Yellott	10/13/1806
	Christ Church	
William & Ann JOHNSON	Loyd	8/1/1807
John & Susanna ASHTON	William	-----
Christ Church	bapt.	Oct 1807

43

Parents	Child	Birth Date
John & Rebecca R. YELLOTT	Mary	4/13/1807
bapt. by Rev. John Allen	Christ Church	
John & Sarah ROUSE	Christopher Chapman	7/27/1807
St. Johns	bapt. at Joppa	11/1/1807
Aaron & Martha MCCOMAS	Calvel	4/12/1807
St. Johns	bapt.	11/11/1807
Abraham & Rachel VAUGHAN	Gist	10/7/1806
Thomas & Mary SUTTON	Dorcas	4/20/1807
David & Mary POCOCK	John	12/4/1806
St. James	bapt.	11/15/1809
Adam & Mary BURNS	Balinda Bull	8/22/1807
Jesse & Jamima HUTCHINS	Elisabeth	10/23/1807
St. James	bapt.	4/12/1808
John & Elisabeth SLADE	Amanda Azana	11/27/1807
Thomas & Sarah SPARKS	Sarah Rampley	3/12/1805
	Elizabeth Ann	7/16/1807
_____ NELSON	John Hutchins	12/1/1807
St. James	bapt.	5/1/1808
Jesse & Catharine POCOCK	Asenath	12/2/1807
John & _____ WILLIAMS	Daniel	7/3/1807
Peacy WILLIAMS	Ely	2/27/1807
Thomas & Elisabeth DAILY	Rachel	9/23/1807
St. James	bapt.	6/6/1808
James & Catharine BATY	William	4/15/1808
Thomas & Christiana _____	Susanna	3/17/1808
St. James	bapt.	6/26/1808
Fayette & Elisabeth JOHNSON	?	
John & Susanna ASHTON	William	5/19/1807
Christ Church		
William & Mary HUTCHINS	Zany Ann	1/28/1808
& Matilda HUTCHINS	Ellen Maria	4/29/1803
St. James - Thomas F. HUTCHINS & Ann HUTCHINS, Sponsors		
Leonard & Jamima ELLIOTT	George	2/22/1807
Joshua & Temperance MARSH	Stephen	2/2/1787
St. James	Rebecca	10/4/1789
	Elijah	10/4/1790
	Grafton	6/13/1792
	Dennis	8/13/1795
	Josiah	6/15/1797
	Ellen	8/17/1799
	Joshua	7/8/1801
	Beale	8/16/1803
	Nelson	3/24/1806
	bapt.	10/1808
John & Rosetta HAMILTON	Thomas	5 years old
St. James	John	5 mos. old
	bapt.	Oct 1808
John & Rebecca R. YELLOT	Elisabeth	9/11/1808
Christ Church		
Gabriel & Mary HOLMES	the child not given in yet	
St. James		
Leonard & Jamima ELLIOTT	Sarah G.	4/1/1809
Samuel & Rachel HUGHES	Aquila	8/17/1808

44

Parents	Child	Birth Date
John & Ann NORRIS	Hannah	7/30/1806
	Mary	8/23/1809
Abraham & Elisabeth ANDERSON	Abraham	12/30/1806
St. James	Joshua	7/13/1809
	bapt.	1809
Abraham & Rachel VAUGHAN	Benjamin	7/2/1809
William & Ann CURTIS	William	8/25/1805
	Eli	?
	Ann	?
Aquila ARMSTRONG	Moses	7/26/1806
John & ____ KEATH	Delila	3/23/1809
Joseph COOPER	Margaret	11/8/1802
	Sophia	4/18/1804
Benjamin STANDIFORD	Sarah H.	11/24/1808
John PICKET	Temperance	3/20/1808
Henry & Comfort WIER	Eveline	3/26/1809
James & Sarah MACORD	Arthur	5/7/1808
	Jesse	?/19/1809
William & Mary DEMOSS	Mary	11/15/1808
David & Mary POCOCK	Jesse	7/8/1809
(Parents names not given)	John Thomas	8/29/1803
	Rebecca Jane	8/9/1807
	James Wiles	2/12/1808
St. James	bapt.	9/29/1809
David & Hannah STREET	John	11/29/1806
Christ Church	bapt.	Nov 1809
William & Nancy RAMPLY	Sarah	8/31/1805
William & Mary HUTCHINS	Sarah	12/23/1809
Peter & Martha BARHAN	Ruth	5/20/1807
	Kinsey	7/21/1809
Jesse & Caterina POCOCK	Juliet Elisabeth	1/29/1810
Dixon & Elisabeth SLADE	Independent	7/11/1804
	Penelope	9/20/1809
Benjamin & Alice ELLIOTT	Elisabeth	7/24/1809
Dickinson & Mary GORSUCH	Mary	9/17/1809
Mordicai & Nancy SUTTON	Micajah	5/5/1810
St. James	bapt.	6/1810
Elijah & Ustinah POCOCK	Catharina	12/11/1808
Joseph & Elisabeth MILLER	Mary	1/4/1810
George & Jemima BOND	Eleanor	7/17/1808
Aaron & Sarah FREELAND	Miranda	10/8/1809
Abraham & Mary FREELAND	John	3/12/1798
St. James	bapt.	7/2/1810
James & Catharine BEATY	Mary Harrimon	11/28/1809
Thomas & Sarah SPARKS	James Rampley	10/29/1809
John & ____ HUTCHINGS	Thomas	12/7/1809
St. James	2 more bapt.	July 1810
Jesse & Jamima HUTCHINGS	William H.	3/5/1810
St. James	bapt.	Aug 1810
William & Hannah GLADDEN	Hannah	1/1/1809
Israel D. & Jane MAULSBY	John Hall	9/20/1808
Christ Church - St. James		July & Aug 1810?

45

Parents	Child	Birth Date
Walter & Elisabeth PERDUE	John	6/29/1804
St. James	Elisabeth	2/19/1807
	Thomas	3/29/1809
William & Mary NORRIS	Susannah	10/3/1800
	Katy	8/16/1805
	at the Manor	May 1811
William & _____ NELSON	Elisabeth Bower	6/12/1810
St. James	(Boner?) bapt.	6/16/1811
Abraham & Margaret ELLIOTT	Maria	9/10/1810
Leonard & Jamima ELLIOTT	Ariel	2/11/1811
St. James	bapt.	July 1811
Samuel & Mary MCMATH	Mary	2/14/1793
Christ Church	bapt.	7/31/1811
Witnesses: Pleasance COLEMAN & Mary JORDAN		
John & Cordelia STANDIFORD	Nicholas John Coleman	2/16/1811
St. James	bapt.	8/25/1811
Josias & Rebecca BULL	Elisha	10/30/1804
	Edward Parish	6/11/1807
	Susanna	2/13/1809
Thomas & Christana RAMPLEY	Sary	1/29/1781
Patren & Jane COLEMAN	Susanna Bull	4/22/1805
Edward & Jemima MORRIS	Lewis	2/12/1810
Frederick & Appelona AYLSROOT	Hannah	1/12/1805
William & Sarah CURRYER	Rachel	1/31/1811
Joseph & _____ BOSLEY	Elisabeth	4/5/1811
Samuel & Rachel HUGHES	Rachel	3/8/1811
Thomas & Elisabeth DAILY	Elisabeth	5/11/1810
Prudence SUTTON	Benjamin Almony	4/16/1811
St. James	bapt.	Sep 1811
John & Rebecca R. YELLOTT	Jeremiah	2/6/1811
George & Bethia YELLOTT	William	2/20/1806
Christ Church	John Jeremiah	10/11/1807
Ezekiel & Nancy SLADE	Armarellen	5/1/1809
	William George	2/8/1811
Archibald & Elisabeth GITTINGS	Nicholas Bosley	4/11/1812
St. James	bapt.	5/3/1812
John & Hannah NELSON	Richard Hutchings	9/9/1811
William & _____ HUTCHINGS	Elisabeth	12/27/1811
Ezekiel & Nancy SLADE	Armarellon	5/1/1809
St. James	William George	2/8/1811
	4 Black children	5/31/1812
Edward & Susanna LEE	Hugh Whiteford	12/29/1811
Christ Church	bapt.	7/5/1812
James & Catharine BATY	Elleanor Flanegan	11/4/1811
William & Sarah SPEARS	Sarah Ann	5/2/1779
	Ann Jamima	3/9/1811
Abraham & Nancy SPRUSBANK	Abraham	3/21/1808
Thomas & Mary RICHARDSON	Jamima Ann	6/24/18??
Jacob & Elisabeth BULL	Hannah Ann	4/15/1812
Joseph & Ruth BURGES	Elisabeth Ellen	6/11/1812
Josias & Comfort ANDERSON	John W.	9/19/1809

Parents	Child	Birth Date
Peter Grubb & Bettcey HUNTER	Pleasant	9/23/1809
St. James	Peter G.	?
	Peter Grubb	bapt 1812
Gest & Rachel VAUGHAN	Gist	9/7/1780
Gest & Charlotte VAUGHN	Emmaline	8/14/1808
	Thomas Norris	4/4/1810
Comfort WIRES		1782
William & Hannah ST. CLAIR	William	7/25/1811
St. James	bapt.	Aug 1812
William & H. GLADDEN	John	6/2/1812
Christ Church	bapt.	8/30/1812
Thomas & Sarah SPARKS	Josias	2/14/1812
Christ Church	bapt.	9/20/1812
Pamelia CLARKE		8/15/1785
	bapt.	10/6/1812
Abraham & Rachel VAUGHAN	James	7/31/1812
Andrew WILSON		6/12/1786
James WILSON		Feb 1784
	bapt.	5/9/1813

Witnesses to above: R. WILSON, Pleasance COLEMAN & Rebecca R. YELLOTT

Parents	Child	Birth Date
Benjamin & Alice ELLIOTT	Delilah Crayton	6/30/1812
Abraham & Margaret ELLIOTT	Sarah White	5/24/1812
Leonard & Jamima ELLIOTT	James Rampley	2/24/1813
William & Martha BOND	John	2/10/1813
St. James	bapt.	May 1813
David & Mary POCOCK	Salome	1/27/1813
St. James		
Joshua & Sarah KILSO	Ariel Hutchins	4/4/1813
____ NELSON	Nicholas Hutchins	12/16/1812
St. James	bapt.	9/5/1813
John HUTCHINS	Nicholas	10/19/1811
son of William -another son	name not remembered	2/25/1813
William & Mary DEMOS	Susanna	8/17/1813
	David	7/22/1811
Thomas & Christian RAMPLEY	Sarah	12/12/1810
	Jamima	1/29/1813
Samuel & Penelope PARKER	Nicholas	5/25/1813
Abraham & Ruth WARE	Mary	11/1/1809
Christ Church		
Thomas & Mary ST. CLAIR	Elisabeth Ruth	7/2/1813
Rogers & Catharine STREETT	Catharine	aged 7 yrs
	Jane	aged 6 yrs
	Belinda	aged 5 yrs
	Rogers	aged 3 yrs
	Nancy	aged 2 yrs
____ KELSO	all bapt.	5/30/1814
William & ____ HUTCHINGS		?
St. James		
John & Hannah NELSON	Sarah	12/15/1813
James & Catharine BEATY	John Demoss	12/9/1813
St. James	bapt.	Aug 1814

Parents	Child	Birth Date
James & Susanna MEADS St. James	John Demoss bapt.	12/19/1813 Aug 1814
Dixon & Martha BROWN St. James	Elizabeth Sarah age abt 3 yrs Mary Ann " " 4 yrs bapt. in D. Brown's private house	8/30/1814
Abraham & Margaret ELLIOTT M. Chh - St. James	Mary Jane bapt.	8/25/1813 10/2/1814
John & R. R. YELLOTT	Charles John bapt. private house	2/21/1815 2/17/1813 Feb 1815
John & Rebecca R. YELLOTT	Mary bapt. by Rev. J. Allen Elisabeth Jeremiah John Charles Coleman bapt. by Rev. M. Johnson George Coleman Thomas Washington bapt. Private Christ Church	4/13/1807 9/11/1808 2/6/1811 2/17/1813 2/21/1815 5/3/1816 7/19/1818 1/19/1821 11/19/1822 9/17/1824 10/22/1794 5/24/1815
Josias WILSON	Elizabeth Ellen	6/15/1815
David & Mary POCOCK	Aquila Carrol William	2/17/1813 3/21/1815
Elisha & ____ GALLOWAY	Ira	8/5/1811
William & Ann CURTIS	Jane Abel	3/17/1810 5/7/1811
Abel & Dinah WALTON	Ann Rebecca private - J. YELLOTTS	5/1/1815 7/30/1815 1815
John Henry & Mary WHEGERS	Joshua Lynch	5/21/1815
Richard & Jemima HUTCHINS	Sarah	7/29/1815
Thomas & Lovisah HUTCHINS	Jamima Hutchins	6/20/1815
Joshua & Sarah KELSEY	Sarah Ann	9/10/1814
Claudius & Susanna HITCHCOCK	Eliza	6/17/1815
William & Ann CURTIS	Rachel Perdue ANDERSON age 1 year 11 months	
Parents names not given -	Ruth ANDERSON	age 3 mo.
Parents names not given -	Ellen Marie CARN born 5/18/1815	
Parents names not given - St. James	Nathaniel bapt.	11/27/1814 10/1/1815
Daniel Dulany & Margaret Murray FITZHUGH	Henry Maynadier bapt. at W. YELLOTTS	6/29/1815 10/25/1815

BURIALS

The following is a list of burials copied by Miss Doris M.
Rowles, of the Historical Records Survey, from a typewritten copy
of the Diary of The Rev. John Coleman, January 15, 1941. They are
not parish records.

1792
Aug. 5 - I preached the funeral for BELINDA AMOS, daughter
          of JAMES & SUSANNA AMOS, Harford Co.
Aug. 30- Buried a child of G. FITZHUGH by name and after preach-
          ing that funeral I read the burial office over two
          children of FLEMMON HILL and his wife ELEANOR; Balti-
          more County, St. James Parish.
Oct. 5 - Buried SAMUEL PILES about 20 yrs. old, son of RALPH
          PILES, Harford County.
 ? -   ROBERT CLARK, St. James Parish, Harford County.
Nov. 3 - WALTER PERDUE of Harford Cty, St. John's Parish, about
          86 yrs.
Nov. 5 - JAMES BUCK, son of CHRISTOPHER BUCK, abt. 5 mos old, BC.
Nov. 17- JOHN BARRETTS, HC, St. James Parish, abt. 50 yrs.
Dec. 5 - MARY HILL, St. James Parish, HC, abt. 50 yrs. old.
Dec. 9 - SARY FLINCHAM, abt. 4 yrs. old, d. of EDWARD FLINCHAM
          & SARAH.
Dec. 16- JOHN WANE, Joppa, abt. 50 yrs. old.

1792
Oct. 22- MR. CROMWELL, BC, St. Thomas, abt. 60 yrs. old.
Oct. 24- JOHN BOND, BC, St. Thomas, 81 yrs. old.

1793
Jany. 1- URATH OWINGS, BC, St. Thomas, 80 yrs.
Jany.24- MRS. JOHNS, BC, St. James, abt. 45 yrs. old.
Feb. 19- AQUILA, son of AQUALA HALL, abt. 3 1/2 or 4 yrs. old,
          BC, St. John's.
Mar. 10- JOHN BOND, Joppa, abt. 27 years old.
Mar. 30- WILLIAM ALLENDER of Deer Creek Chapel, abt. 50.
Apr. 4 - ELIZABETH JOLLY, Deer Creek Chapel, abt. 50.
Apr. 12- JOHN LOVE, Esquire, HC, abt. 61 or 62 yrs. old.
May 5 - SARAH DAVIES, Joppa, a widow.
Jun. 23- The widow NORRIS, St. James Parish, BC.
Jul. 7 - HORATIO HUGHES, St. James, abt. 40 yrs. old.
Jul. 14- MARY BAZTER, St. John's Parish, abt. 40 yrs. old.
 ?   MARGARET ROBINSON, St. John's Parish, abt. 60.
Aug. 4 - WALTER PERDUE's child, St. James Parish.
Aug. 8 - PENELOPE STANSBURY, St. James, abt. 17 yrs. of age.
Aug. 21- SARAH RICHARDSON, abt. 8 yrs. old.
Sep. 7 - THOMAS HOPKINS, abt. 70 yrs. old.
Sep. 16- MARY WILMOTT, abt. 75 yrs. old.
Oct. 8 - JOHN BUCK, aged abt. 72, BC, St. John's Parish.
Oct. 12- WILIAM ROE, abt. 57 and MARY ROE, abt. 30, St. James.
Oct. 13- JOHN SHEPHERD, Jun., abt. 42 yrs. old, St. James Parish.
Oct. 27- WILLIAM STANDIFORD, abt. 53, St. James Parish.
Oct. 30- MRS. BUCK, abt. 70 yrs. old, St. John's Parish.
Nov. 3 - REBECCA WRIGHT of HC, Joppa, abt. 37 years old.
Nov. 4 - JAMES WARD, HC, St. John's Parish, abt. 60 vrs. old.

BURIALS

1793
Nov. 15- JACOB ALBERT, Sen. abt. 70, HC, St.George Parish.
Nov. 16-   MCCOMAS, abt. 19 yrs. old, HC.
Nov. 17- JOHN GRIFFIN, 3 mos old, a child, at the old furnace.
Nov. 18-   BAKER, wife of JAMES BAKER, HC, same day a child
             in the same grave with the mother. MCCOMAS,
             St. John's Parish; FORWOOD, St. George's Parish.

1794
Jan. 25- STEPHEN OWINGS, aged abt. 43 yrs., St. James Parish.
Jan. 17- JAMES FRANKLIN, aged abt. 60, St. James Parish.
Feb. 12- Capt. WILLIAM BRADFORD, aged abt. 55, St. John's.
Feb. 13- THOMAS DURHAM, aged abt. 66, St. John's Parish.
Feb. 15- JAMES MCCOMAS, St. James Parish, abt. 38 years.
Feb. 19- HANNAH KEMP, St. John's Parish, abt. 70 years old.
Mar. 2 - JOHN THOMAS BROWN, St. John's Parish, abt. 28 yrs. old.
Mar. 3 -   MATHERS, St. John's Parish, abt. 76 yrs. old.
Mar. 21- HUGH DEVER (?) HC, St. George's Parish, aged abt. 48.
Mar. 24- MOSES MCCOMAS, St. John's Parish, aged abt. 53.
May 4 - BENJAMIN HUGHES)
            MARTHA WHEELER) St. James Parish.
May 5 -   MORRIS of St. James Parish, aged abt. 72.
May 11 - JOHN GRIFFIN, Sen., St. John's Parish, aged abt. 65.
Jun. 2 - FREDERICK SWANN, St. James Parish, aged abt. 60.
Jun. 22- ABRAHAM NORRIS, St. John's Parish, 4 years & 8 months.
Jul. 27- NATHANAEL BRYARLY, St. James Parish, aged 30.
            The same day, ABRAHAM GUYTON's child, 6 years.
Jul. 29- Died & was buried soon after, JOHN CURTIS, abt. 8 yrs.
Jul. 30- Died & was buried soon after PENELOPE ANDERSON, abt. 7
            yrs. old.
Aug. 3 - Died & was buried the same day with the two above,
            DANIEL CURTIS, abt. 1p (sic) years old, BC, St. James.
Aug. 10-   JONES, dau. of RICHARD JONES.
Sep. 2 - ELLENOR MERRYMAN, St. James Parish, aged abt. 14.
Sep. 4 - BENJAMIN FRANKLIN & THOMAS FRANKLIN, St. James Parish.
Sep. 14- AQUILA HOWARD & NANECY HOWARD, St. John's Parish, abt. 6
            or 7 yrs. old.
Sep. 20- LESTER SYMILEAR (?) buried St. James Parish, abt. 50
            yrs. old.
Nov.1794-EDMOND TALBOTT died Nov. 1794 & was buried 25th, aged 88
            yrs., HC.
Nov.1794-Two children of   FUGATE at the M Church.
Dec. 10- ELEAZER BRYERLY, abt. 47 yrs. old, HC.
Dec. 14- WILLIAM ANDERSON, aged abt. 50 yrs., M Ch yard.

1795
Feb. 18- DANIEL MCCOMAS, aged abt. 74, St. John's Parish.
Feb. 19- WILLIAM SLADE, St. James Parish.
Feb. 20- WILLIAM WILSON, aged abt. 3 years, St. John's Parish.
Feb. 22- SARAH MOORES, aged abt. 40, St. John's Parish.
Mar. 30- THOMAS BOND, aged abt. 56, St. John's Parish, Middle
            River Neck.
May 26 -   HUNTER, abt. 13 yrs. old, St. James Parish.
Jun. 11- HANNAH TAYLOR, abt. 25 yrs. old, St. John's Parish.

BURIALS

1795
Jun. 28- RICHARD BRYARLY, abt. 30 & HENRY BRYARLY, abt. 40, St.
         James Parish.
Sep. 19- LEAH HARTLEY, abt. 30, St. John's Parish.
Sep. 20- A child of Mr. SLADE, abt. 3 yrs. old, St. James Parish.
         The same day, Mrs. LYTLE,wife of GEORGE LYTLE, St. James
Oct. 3 - THOMAS SMITHSON, Sen., abt. 83 yrs. old, St. John's.
Oct. 5 - A child of JOHN CHANIER (?) abt. 11 yrs. old, St. Johns.
Oct. 16- GEORGE FITZHUGH's child, St. James Parish, abt. 6 yrs.
         old.
Oct. 22- Dr. J. NICHOLSON's child, abt. 7 months old.
Oct. 23- SAMUEL WATKINS, aged 70 or upwards.
Nov. 19- JAMES GITTINGS, Jun., child abt. 3 yrs. old, St. John's.
Nov. 25- SALLY AMOS, abt. 3 yrs. old, St. John's.
Nov. 28- MORDIAI (?) AMOS, Sen. wife, St. James Parish.

1796
Feb. 14- ELIZABETH ROBINET, St. John's Parish (Joppa).
Apr. 6 - JOHN GORSUCH, 81 yrs. old, St. James Parish.
Apr. 25- EDWARD FLANNAGAN, abt. 45, St. John's Parish.
May   6 - HARRY GREEN's child, abt. 8 months old.
May 14 - HARRY, son of THOMAS and ANN WRIGHT, abt. 3 months old.
May 28 - WILLIAM MORGAN, Deer Creek Chapel, abt. 58 yrs. old.
Jun. 6 - BENJAMIN MERRYMAN, BC, St. James Parish, 30 yrs.
Aug. 26- Mrs. DAY, abt. 60 yrs. old, St. John's Parish.
Sep. 18- JOSHUA BOND, an infant, son of THOMAS BOND.
Nov. 15- MOSES JOHNSON of St. James Parish, aged abt. 65.
Nov. 21- MARY CHAMBERS, St. John's Parish, aged abt. 56.
?   ANN MERRYMAN, St. James Parish.

1797
Jan. 10- WILLIAM STEWARD, St. James Parish, abt. 40 yrs. old.
Feb. 3 - SARAH of JOHN & MATILDA NICHOLSON, St. James Parish.
Mar. 29-   GRAHAME, buried at Belle Air, aged abt. 55.
Mar. 30- AQUILA HALL, aged abt. 2 years, St. John's.
Apr. 20- JOHN RUTLEDGE STANDIFORD &)
Apr. 24- SKELTON STANDIFORD   )
May 13- ROBERT CLARK, aged abt. 60, HC.
May 29- ELIZABETH MILLER, aged abt. 30, BC.
Jun. 7 - JOSHUA ELENOS (?), abt. 18 months old.
         SOLOMON ELENOS (?) abt. 2 months old, BC.
Jun. 24- JOHN THOMAS, aged abt. 46, HC, Deer Creek.
Jun. 25-   GORSUCH, aged 26, BC.
Aug. 18- JOHN WHITTAKER, aged abt. 4 yrs., St. John's Parish.
Aug. 20- EDWARD BOZMAN, aged abt. 30, St. James.
Aug. 30- BARBARA MCCAUSLAND, aged 77.
Aug. 31- WILLIAM TRAPNELL, aged 83.
Sep. 1 - JOHN HARE, aged one year & 10 months.
         Another child same day at M Ch, CHARITY POCOCK, 10
         months old.
Sep. 3 - JOSHUA FLAHERTY, aged 56.
Sep. 4 - Dr. AQUILLA DURHAM, abt. 25 yrs. old.
Oct. 17- ANN DURHAM buried, aged about 57.
Nov. 19- JOHN DAY, two years old, son of Dr. DAY.

BURIALS

1798
Mar. 10- JOSHUA BUCK, aged 15 yrs., St. John's.
Mar. 31- JOSHUA GREEN, aged 18 months, died Feb. 6/98.
Apr. 15- Daughter of DAVID & S. POCOCK, aged two years.
Apr. 26- SKELTON STANDIFORD, born Nov. 1700, dec'd and buried
         April 26, 1798, St. James.
         PENELOPE RICHARDSON, aged abt. 23 years.
Jun. 8 - THOMAS JOHNSON, of Thos., aged abt. 50 years.
Jun.1798-A son of HUGH YOUNG, abt. 4 years old.
Jun. 17- The widow JARVIS, aged about 65.
Jun. 24- JOHN ALMONY, aged about 30 years.
Jul. 8 - ELEANOR ADDISON HOLLIDAY, aged abt. 46.
1798   JOHNSON, a young child of DAVID JOHNSON.
Fall 1798 - SAMUEL DAY, aged abt. 70 years.

1799
Jan. 12- JAMES GROOMBRIDGE, aged 77, St. James Parish, BC.
Jan. 20- BENJAMIN RUMSEY, Jun., aged 24, Joppa.
Jan. 30- ELIZABETH G. SMITH, aged abt. 7 mo., BC, St. Johns.
Apr. 6 - _____ KEITH, aged 103 years, St. James Parish.
July - ELIJAH MERRYMAN, aged 45 or 6, St. James Parish.
Jul. 10- SUSANNA HUDSON, aged 46, St. Thomas Parish.
Jul. 21- MICHAEL WOLF, aged abt. 65, St. Thomas Parish.
Aug. 20- CATHERINE BUCK, aged abt. 30, St. John's Parish.
Sep. 3 - WILLIAM STONE, aged abt. 14 yrs., St. Thomas Parish.
Sep. 23- H. STANSBURY, aged 98 yrs. near Towson's tavern.
Sep. 26- PENELOPE RUTLEDGE, aged abt. 70 yrs., St. James, BC.
Nov. 6 - CATHARINE ROGERS, aged 86, St. Thomas Parish, BC.
Dec. 2 - ELIZABETH TOLLEY, aged abt. 14, St. John's Parish.

1800
Jan. 15- BLANCH HOWARD, St. John's Parish, aged abt. 58.
Jan. 29- ELIZABETH MERRYMAN, aged 24, St. James Parish.
Apr. 28- DANIEL POCOCK, aged 80 yrs., St. James Parish.
Apr. 30- REBECCA BLANEY, aged abt. 23 yrs., St. James Parish.
         Mrs. _____ WARD, widow, aged abt. 52, St. James
         Parish.
         Major GEST (?) VAUGHAN, aged abt. 68, St. James Parish.
Jun. 29- FREDERICK CRISTMAN, aged 23 years, 6 months, St. Thomas
         Parish.
Jul. 7 - JOHN ROBERT HOLLIDAY, aged 55, St. Thomas Parish.
Jul. 13- Mrs. _____ COLE, aged 45, buried St. Thomas Chh yd.
Aug. 27- JOHN RUTLEDGE, aged 47, St. James Parish.
Sep. 3 - _____ GRIFFIN, aged abt, 23, St. Thomas.
Sep. 27- WILLIAM SEMMES, aged 27, St. Thomas Parish.
Oct. 24- SUSANNA GEST, aged 86, St. Thomas Parish.
Nov. 6 - ELIAS BROWN, aged abt. 45, St. Thomas Parish.
Nov. 11- Mrs. HICKS, abt. 52, St. James Parish.
Nov. 12- HENRY SCARFF, aged 82 yrs., St. James Parish.
Nov. 22- A child of DARBY & MARY LUX, St. James Parish.
Nov. 24- SARAH DAUVIDGE MERRYMAN departed this life 20 Oct. 1800,
         aged 37, St. James.
Nov. 25- THOMAS STREET, aged 43, St. James.
Dec. 26- Mrs. _____ SLADE, aged about 30, St. James Parish.

52

BURIALS

1801
Feb. 1p- JOSHUS MERRYMAN, born 17 Apr. 1768, died 27 Jany. 1801,
(sic)   St. James Parish.
Mar. 20- ARCHIBALD GITTINGS, born Jany. 16 1799, son of JAMES
         GITTINGS, Jun., St. James or St. John's Parish.
Apr. 6 - MARTHA MERRYMAN was born 31 day July 1781, died 19 Mar.
         1801, St. James Parish.
May   4 - SOLOMON ARMSTRONG, aged 78, St. James.
May   - JOHN ELLIOTT, abt. 65, St. James Parish.
May   3 - ELIZABETH BOYLES, aged abt. 62, St. James.
Jun. 8 - THOMAS WARE, aged 88, St. James Parish.
Jul. 10- JOHN CROXALL's child ELLINOR, 6 months old, St. Thomas
         Parish.
Jul. 12- MARY SIMMONS, aged 24, St. Thomas.
Jul. 24- NICHOLAS MERRYMAN, Senr., aged 75 or 6, died July 14 &
         buried July 24, 1801, St. James Parish, BC.
Aug. 7 - THOMAS MARSH and Mrs. MARSH his wife, aged about 80,
         St. James Parish.
Sep. 1 - Mrs. TALLEY, aged abt. 82 years, St. John's.
Sep. 4 - ELIZABETH VAUGHAN, aged 21 years, St. James.
Oct. 1 - MARGARET WALKER, aged 64, St. Margaret's Westminster
         Parish, AC.
Oct. 2y- HENRY SUTTON, eldest son of JOSEPH SUTTON, aged abt.
(sic)   45, St. James.
Oct. 28- ELIAKIM JAMES, aged 35.
Nov. 7 - EZEKIEL BOSLEY, aged abt. 63, St. James Parish.
Dec. 24- ANDREW WICORT (?), aged abt. 50, St. Thomas Parish.
Dec. 28- THOMAS ANDERSON, aged abt. 50, St. James Parish.

1802
Jan. 5 - EDMOND STANSBURY, aged abt. 55.)
         ELIZABETH TALBOTT, aged abt. 30.) St. James Parish.
May   - ASINA SHREEVE, aged abt. 25, St. Thomas.
Jun. 8 -   LOVE, dau. of JOHN LOVE, aged abt. 38, St.
         George's Parish.
June   - Mrs. ANN JOHNSON, aged abt. 57, St. Thomas.
Aug.   - Doctor JOHNSON's child, abt. 12 months old.
Aug. 28- Mrs.   MERRYMAN, aged abt. 80 yrs., St. James.
Sep. 2 - J. SLADE, aged 79, St. James.
Sep. 27- NICHOLAS MERRYMAN's child, aged abt. 4 years.
Nov. 22- WALTER FITZHUGH, aged abt. 29, son of G.F., St. James.

1803
Feb. 11- Mrs. TIMANUS, St. Thomas.
Apr. 9 -   SHEPPARD, son of the widow SHEPPARD, St.
         James.

1803
Apr. 25- ROBERT LOVE, son of JOHN LOVE, aged 24, St. George's
         Parish or St. John's; died 3 Nov. 1802.
Jun. 8 - ELIZABETH JACKSON, aged abt. 7 years, St. Thomas Parish.
Jun. 12- SAMUEL OWINGS, aged 69 & 10 months, St. Thomas.
Jun. 27- RALPH PYLE, aged 75, St. George's Parish.
Jul. 4 - THOMAS ANDERSON, aged 75, St. James.
? 1803 - THOMAS G. HOWARD, aged abt. 60, St. John's.

BURIALS

Oct. 10- _____, d. of JOHN CROXALL, aged 6 months, St.
          Thomas.
Nov. 22- NATHANAEL R. RAWLINGS, aged abt. 30, St. Thomas.
Dec. 4 - DANIEL HUDSON, aged abt. 47, St. Thomas.

1804
Jan. 17- FANNY POCOCK, 41 yrs. old, St. James.
Feb. 5 - JACOB WAGGONER, abt. 28 yrs. old, buried Feb. 5, St.
          Thomas. Same day his child buried who.died a few days
          before.
Apr. 19- SARAH PYLE, aged abt. 70, St. Georges'
May 6 - HANNAH FULTON , aged abt. 71, St. John's.
May 8 - Mrs. JOHNSON, aged abt. 73, St. George's.
May 20 - THOMAS WELLS, aged 95, St. Thomas Parish.
June 17- ELIZA HULSE, aged 63, St. Thomas Parish.
Sep. 28- THOMAS GITTINGS, aged 42, St. Thomas.
Sep. 30- SUSANNA HUTCHINGS, aged 18, St. James.
Sep. 30- GEORGE GITTINGS, aged 18, St. James.

1805
Feb. 19- ELEANOR CROXALL, aged 75, St. Thomas.
Mar. 1 - JOHN BEALE HOWARD, aged 95, St. John's.
Mar. 20- WILLIAM ANDERSON, aged 51, St. James Parish.
Apr. 9 - JAMES AMOS Sen., aged 82, St. James.
May 2 - WILLIAM DIMMIT, aged abt. 60, St. John's.
Sep. 17- MARY THOMAS, aged abt. 55.
 1805 - RUTH SHEETS, aged abt. 30, St. Thomas Parish.
 1805 - Mrs. _____ SAMPSON, aged abt. 70, St. James.
May   - JOHN HALL, aged abt. 50.
No date- A child of GIDEON WILSON's abt. 5 yrs. old, St. James.

1806
Mar. 23- JOHN DEMOSS (?), Sen., 89 yrs. old, St. James.
Apr. 8 - MARY ANDERSON, aged 98, St. James.
Apr. 7 - JOHN CILLINGHAM, aged abt. 55, St. James.
Mar. 3 - PRISCILLA FULTON, aged 45,St. John's, HC.
May 18- JOHN MARSH, aged abt. 48, BC.
Apr. 20- BENJAMIN VAUGHAN, aged abt. 30, St. James.
June   - ANN YELLOTT WILLIAMS, aged abt. 5 yrs., Christ Church,HC.
Jul. 14- JOHN STAHDIFORD, aged abt. 65,St. James Parish.
June   - RUTH RIDGELEY, aged abt. 30, St. James Parish.
Jul. 22- Mrs. PIERCE, wife of THOMAS P., aged abt. 36.
Nov.   - ----- HENDON, aged 70, St. John's or St. James.
No date - T. GAZAWAY HOWARD, aged abt. 35, St. James.
Nov. 6 - SUSANNA HUTCHINGS, aged 70, St. James.
Nov. 1 - WALTERA [sic] PAUL, aged 75, St. John's Parish.

1807
Nov. 11- Mrs. MCCOMAS, aged abt. 60, St. John's Parish.

1808
Apr. 12- AQUILA MILES, aged abt. 35, St. James Parish.
Apr. 13- SOLOMON WADLEY, aged 2 yrs. & 3 months, St. James.
May 15 - MICHAEL WILLITT, aged abt. 30, St. James.
May 16 - EDWARD RUTLEDGE, aged abt. 28, St. James.

Nov. 3 - RALPH THOMAS, aged abt. 26, Christ Church HC.
Dec. 5 - SAMUEL RICHARDSON, aged abt. 38, St. James.
Dec. 5 - Widow RICHARDSON, St. James.

1809
Sep. 10- Two children of JOSHUA HUTCHINGS, St. James.
Sep. 11- ELIZABETH LEACH, aged 81, St. James.
Sep. 24- Mrs. _____ WILEY, aged abt. 70, St. James.
Sep.   -   COX, aged abt. 3 years, St. James.
Oct.   - Widow BLANEY, aged abt. 70, Christ Church or St. James.
 1809 - _____ HUTCHINGS, a young man about 23.

1810
Jun. 3 - _____ ELLIOTT, aged abt. 25, St. James.
Jun. 3 - JOSEPH SUTTON, aged abt. 84, St. James
Jul. 2 - CHARLES BOND, aged abt. 30, St. James.
Sep. 9 - _____, a young woman abt. 19.
Sep. 23- SAMUEL GWYNN, aged 22, St. James.
Oct. 14- MARTHA ST. CLAIR, aged 64.

ADAMS, Elisabeth 4, 39
  Hannah 39
  John 39
  Sarah 39
ADDISON, John Jr. 3
  Sarah (LERTCH) 3
ADY, Joshua 3
  Mary (FORD) 3
AILSROD, Appelona 42
  Bilinda 42
  Frederick 42
AIRS, Elizabeth 18
  Jeremiah 18
  Joshua 18
  Mary 8
  Sarah 18
  Thomas 18
ALBERT, Jacob 50
  Mary 1
ALDRIDGE, Elisabeth 7
ALEXANDER, Rebecca (HAYS) 2
  Robert 2
ALFREED, Abilena 13
  Frederick 13
  Rachel 13
  Susanna 13
ALLEN, Ann 7
  Catharine 28
  Elisabeth (HOPKINS) 7
  J. 48
  James 28
  John 7, 28
  Robert 7
ALLENDER, John Wane 29
  William 29, 49
ALMONY, Ann 38, 41
  Benjamin 38
  Elisabeth 41
  James 38
  John 38, 41, 52
AMOS, Ann 33
  Belinda 49
  Benjamin 33
  Cassandra 10
  Daniel 33
  Elisabeth 27, 33
  Elisabeth Baldwin 37
  Gabriel 13
  George 10
  Hannah 7, 24
  Henry R. 42
  James 27, 49
  James Sr. 54
  John Johnson 33
  John Street 42

AMOS, Julianna 38
  Levi 33
  Martha 13, 33
  Mary 10, 42
  Mary Ann 33
  Mordecai 24, 27
  Mordiai 51
  Philip 33
  Rachel 27
  Robert 13, 33
  Robert Clark 33
  Ruth 38
  Sally 51
  Sarah 33
  Scott 29
  Susanna 27, 33, 37, 49
  Temperance 29
  Thomas 24, 29
  Vincent 24
  William 38
  Zachariah 33, 37
AMOSS, Anna 5
  Benjamin 19
  Elizabeth 19
  James 19
  Martha 19
  Mordecai 19
  Robert 19
  Susanna 19
  William 19
ANDERSON, Abraham 17, 32, 39, 45
  Abraham G. 32
  Ann 32, 39
  Cassandra 4
  Comfort 43, 45
  Cordelia 32
  Elijah 14
  Elisabeth 32, 45
  Elizabeth 17
  Ira 32
  Jesse 10
  John 9, 17
  John W. 46
  Joshua 9, 32, 45
  Josias 43, 46
  Juliet Elisabeth 32
  Leonard 14
  Martha 10
  Mary 32, 54
  Nathan 9
  Penelope 12, 50
  Rachel 9, 43
  Rachel Perdue 48
  Rosannah 17
  Ruth 12, 14, 32, 48

56

ANDERSON, Sarah 5, 39
  Thomas 12, 14, 32, 53
  William 32, 50, 54
ANDOEUL, Christopher 17
  Joseph 17
  Margaret 17
  Rebecca 17
  Susanna 17
ANDREW, Christopher 17
  Joseph 17
  Margaret 17
  Mary 31
  Priscilla 31
  Rebecca 17
  Susanna 17
  William 31
ARMSTRONG, Alice 31, 40, 41
  Aquila 31, 40, 41, 45
  Elisabeth 40
  Moses 45
  Sarah 31
  Solomon 41, 53
ARVIN, Elizabeth (HARDCASTLE) 1
  William 1
ASHTON, Hannah 43
  James 10, 18
  John 43, 44
  Joseph 43
  Mary 10, 18
  Susanna 43, 44
  William 43, 44
ASKEW, Betsey 28
  Derumple 28
  Elisabeth 28
  Sarah (CALWELL) 5
  William 5
ASQUITH, David 3
  Frances (NICHOLS) 3
ATKINSON, Hannah (BURNET) 7
  Isaac 7
AUSTIN, Hannah 11
  Isaac 13
  James 11
  Lawless 13
  Mary 11
AYLSROOT, Appelona 46
  Frederick 46
  Hannah 46
AYRES, Elisabeth 22, 32, 33, 38
  Henry 35
  James 22
  Mary 23
  Matilda 37
  Rachel 23, 37
  Samuel 32

AYRES, Sarah 35
  Susanna 32
  Thomas 22, 23, 32, 33, 37, 38
AYRS, Elizabeth 12
  Rosanna 12
  Stephen 12
BACON, Mary 4
BAGLEY, Susannah (HUSBANDS) 2
  William 2
BAHEN, Elisabeth 42
  Martha 42
  Peter 42
BAILEY, John 33
  Rebecca 33
  Ruth 5
  Thomas 33
BAILY, Rachel (PRESTON) 7
  William 7
BAKER, Belinda (BOSLEY) 2
  Cordelia 5
  James 50
  Nathan 2
BALLARD, Rebecca 29
  Robert 29
  William 29
BALMER, George 35
  Margaret 35
BARHAN, Kinsey 45
  Martha 45
  Peter 45
  Ruth 45
BARNHARROW, Ann 42
  Francis 42
  Mary 42
BARNHOUSE, Ann 17, 40
  Francis 17, 30, 40
  John 17
  Nancy 30, 40
  Thomas 30
  William 40
BARNLEY, Ann 26
  Arthur 26
  John 26
BARNY, Eleanor 16
  Rhoda 16
  Thomas 16
BARRETTS, John 49
BARTON, Ann 3, 27, 30
  Asael 3, 21, 27
  Eleanor 31
  Elisabeth 30, 38
  James 12, 30
  John 12
  Margaret 30
  Margaret Wodden 21

BARTON, Mary 3, 30, 31, 38
  Milly 12
  Nancy Wilson 21
  Robert 38
  Susanna 21, 27
  Susannah (MILLIKIN) 3
  Thomas 31
  Thomas Smithson 30
  William Wilson 21
BARY, Bennet 16
  Charles 16
  Margaret 16
BASHAM, Martha 40
  Matilda 40
  Peter 40
BATEMAN, Henry 15
  Lemuel 15
BATTEN, Dorothea 1
BATY, Catharine 44, 46
  Elleanor Flanegan 46
  James 44, 46
  William 44
BAXTER, Isabella 21
  John 21
  M. 21
  Mary 21
  Sarah 5
BAYLES, Augustine 20
  Elizabeth 20
  Martha D. 20
  Nimrod 20
BAYLEY, Sarah 2
BAYREY, Charles 13
  Elizabeth 13
  Margaret 13
BAZTER, Mary 49
BEATY, Ann 39
  Catharine 45, 47
  Catharine (DEMOSS) 7
  James 7, 45, 47
  John 39
  John Demoss 47
  Mary Harrimon 45
  William 39
BELT, Catharine 14, 16
  Grafton 8
  Horatio 14, 16
  Mary Grafton 14
  Thomas Hanson 14
  Walter Delany 16
BEMER, Barbara 4
BEVARD, Rececca 39
  William 39
BEWARD, Martha 1
BIDDISON, Ann 31

BIDDISON, Daniel 23
  Kirenhappuck 17, 23, 31
  Meshach 17
  Meshack 31
  Mesick 23
  Salam 17
  Shadrack 31
BIDDLE, Augustine 3
BIDISON, Abraham 14
  Caranhappock 14
  Meshack 14
BIRKHEAD, Elisabeth (WATERS) 5
  Thomas 5
BISHOP, Bothier 22
  Elijah 22
  Esther 22
  Jemima 22
  Rebecca 22
  William 22
BIVEN, Ellenor 28
  James 28
  Joshua 28
BLANEY, Ann 7
  Rebecca 52
  Ruth 8
  Widow 55
BLAYDON, Mary 6
BLEANY, Josiah 39
  Mary 39
  Melissey 39
BOEN, Catharine 30
  Elisha 30
  Rebecca 30
  Robert 30
BOISE, Eleanor 16
  John 16
  Mary 16
  Rebecca 16
  Thomas 16
BOND, Alice 26
  Ann (TALBOTT) 3
  Barnet 18
  Cassandra Lee (MORGAN) 5
  Charles 55
  Dennis 13, 18
  Eleanor 45
  Elisabeth 37
  Elisha 39
  Eliza 2
  George 39, 45
  Hannah (HUGHES) 5
  Harriott 13
  Jamimi 39
  Jane 18, 37
  Jemima 45

BOND, John 47, 49
  Joshua 26, 51
  Josias 18
  Martha 47
  Mary 13, 18, 26
  Mordicai 5
  Peggy 4
  Ralph 37
  Salley Charity 4
  Sarah 18, 26
  Thomas 3, 26, 50, 51
  Tobias 26
  William 18, 47
  Zacchens Onion 5
BORN, Catharine 30
  Elisha 30
  Rebecca 30
  Robert 30
BOSELY, Mary 29
  Bazil 4
  Belinda 2
  Charles 22
  Elijah 1
  Elisabeth 6, 29, 35, 38, 40, 46
  Elizabeth (HUTCHINS) 4
  Ezekiel 53
  Hannah 40, 42
  Hannah (HUGHES) 6
  Hannah (WILMOT) 1
  Isaac 4, 29, 35, 38
  James 6, 40, 42
  Joseph 38, 43, 46
  Letice 38
  Letty 43
  Mary 22, 43
  Nancey 42
  Nicholas 38
  Prudence 15
  Rebecca (CHAMBERLIN) 4
  Susanna 5
  Walter 22
BOTTS, Sarah 3
BOWEN, Benjamin 22
  Catharine 22, 30
  Elisha 22, 30
  John 30
  Josias 22
  William 30
BOWERS, Hannah (BRONWELL) 4
  John 4
BOWLER, Peter 1
  Rachel (COEN) 1
BOWMAN, Benjamin 25
  Henry 25
  John 25

BOWMAN, Rachel 25
BOYLES, Deliah 37
  Elizabeth 53
  Margaret 37
BOZMAN, Edward 51
BRADFORD, Martha 1
  Sarah 2
  William 50
BRADLEY, Clary 31
  Edward 31
  Hannah Rutledge 32
  Mary 31
  Sarah 32
  Susanna 31
BRADY, Elisabeth 32
  James 32
  Ruth 32
BRANNIAN, John 2
  Sarah (GEORGE) 2
BRIERLY, Ann 12
  George 12
BRINLEY, Magdalene 24
  Nathan 24
  Nathaniel 24
BRONWELL, Hannah 4
BROWN, Ann 35
  Dixon 48
  Elias 35, 52
  Elizabeth 13
  Elizabeth Sarah 48
  Fanny 28
  George 13, 28
  Hannah (MURRY) 4
  John Thomas 50
  Joshua 35
  Martha 48
  Mary 35
  Mary Ann 48
  Prudence Ann 35
  Rebecca 13
  Thomas 4
BROWNLEY, Catharine 19
  E. F. 19
  Elisabeth 19
  James Stewart 19
  John Smith 19
  Joseph 19
  Thomas Archer 19
BRUSBANKS, Abraham 34
  Ann 34
  Mary 34
  William 34
BRYARLY, Ann 12, 17
  Appiah 41
  David 9

BRYARLY, Deliverance 34
  Elisabeth 25, 37
  Elizabeth 17
  George 17
  Hannah 40
  Henry 25, 51
  Isabella 25
  James 10
  Jane 12
  Jonathan Lyon 25
  Margaret 25
  Mary Ann 29
  Nathanael 50
  Richard 51
  Robert 9, 10, 12, 17, 25, 29,
    34, 37, 40, 41
  Sarah 9, 10, 25, 29, 34, 37,
    40, 41
  Susanna 17
  Thomas 9, 17
BRYCE, Margaret 4
BRYERLY, Eleazer 50
BUCHANAN, Andrew 37
  Ann 37
  Dorothea 37
BUCK, Benjamin 28
  Benjamin Merryman 31
  Catharine 31
  Catharine (MERRYMAN) 4
  Catherine 52
  Chloe 9
  Christopher 28, 31, 49
  Dorcas 27
  James 33, 49
  John 4, 31, 49
  Joshua 9, 31, 33, 52
  Kezia 31
  Kizia 28
  Mrs. 49
  Sarah 9, 33
BUCKANAN, Sarah 2
BUDD, Sarah 3
BULL, Anna 24
  Balinda 35
  Betsey Ann 33
  Christopher 29
  Cordelia 19
  Edward Parish 46
  Elisabeth 29, 46
  Elisha 46
  Elizabeth 19
  Hannah 5
  Hannah Ann 46
  Jacob 9, 13, 46
  John 19, 29, 40

BULL, Josiah 35
  Josias 24, 46
  Josias S. 40
  Josias Slade 33, 37
  Margaret 9
  Mary 9
  Pamelia 31
  Rebecca 24, 33, 35, 37, 40, 46
  Ruth 12
  Sarah 9, 12, 22, 31
  Susanna 46
  Walter 12, 22, 31
  Walter Billingsly 12
  William 19
BURGES, Catheenah 12
  Elisabeth Ellen 46
  Joseph 12, 46
  Ruth 46
BURK, Elisabeth 27
  James 27
  Margaret 27
BURN, Adam 18, 24
  Jacob 21
  Magdalene 18, 24
  Mary 21
  Michael 21
  Sarah 18
  Stephen 24
BURNET, Hannah 7
  Hannah (SPENCER) 1
  John 1
BURNS, Adam 13, 33, 38, 44
  Andrew 1
  Belinda Bull 44
  Catharine 42
  Jacob 13
  John 33
  Magdalene 13
  Mary 13, 33, 34, 35, 38, 42, 44
  Mary (BUSSEY) 1
  Michael 13, 34, 35, 42
  Rachel 34
  Sarah 34
  Susanna 35
  William Bull 38
BURTON, Ann 4
  Constant 27
  Delia 27
  Joseph 27
  Pleasance 27
  Ruth 5
BUSSEY, Mary 1
BUTLER, Richard 3
  Sarah (BOTTS) 3
BYFORD, Henry 2, 12

BYFORD, Mary 12
  Mary (MCCLURE) 2
  William 12
BYRNS, Elizabeth 16
  Magdalene 16
CAIERNS, James 43
  John 43
  Mary 43
CALDER, John 33, 37
  Matilda 37
  Nancy 37
  Naomi 33
  Sophia 33
CALGAL, Daniel 20
  Henry 20
  Rastes 20
  Susanna 20
CALWELL, Sarah 5
CAMPBELL, Eleanor 1
CANOLE, Charles 22
  Ruth 22
CARLILE, Ann 18
  James 18
  Lancelot 18
CARLIN, Elizabeth 10
  Joseph 10
  Robert 10
CARLISLE, Ann 39
  Lancelott 39
  Larkin 39
CARLTON, John 36
  Mary 36
  William 36
CARN, Ellen Marie 48
CARR, Daniel 35
  Elisabeth Ann 35
  Frances 14
  John 14
  Margaret 2, 14
  Milcah (MERRYMAN) 7
  Sarah 14
  Susanna 35
  Thomas 7
CARROL, John 11
CARROLL, Amelia 26
  Benjamin 3, 26
  Delia 6
  Milly (PROCTON) 3
  Sarah 26
CARTY, Francis 3
  Magdalane (JUEL) 3
CATREL, Mary 9
  William 9
  William Regden 9
CHALK, Mary 36

CHALK, Nathan 36
  Zaccariah 36
CHAMBERLAIN, Elizabeth 15
  John 15
  Philip 15
  Samuel 15
  Susanna 5
  Thomas 15
  William 15
CHAMBERLIN, Rebecca 4
CHAMBERS, Mary 51
CHANCE, Frances 27
  John 11, 27
  Martha 11, 27
  Sarah 11
  Wealthian 27
CHAPMAN, Ann (SYKES) 6
  Job 6
CHARLTON, Catharine 37
  John 37
  Mary 37
CHEW, Elizabeth (MORGAN) 2
  Thomas Sheredine 2
CHINE, Mary 2
CHINWORTH, Elisabeth 23
  Rachel (NORRIS) 1
  Susanna 23
  Thomas 1
  William 23
CHURCHMAN, Enoch 3
  Martha (NORRIS) 3
CILLINGHAM, John 54
CLARK, Ann 39
  Barnet 30
  Barnet Johnson 41
  Cassandra (ANDERSON) 4
  Daniel 26
  Dorcas 19
  George 26, 31
  Hester 31
  John 4
  Mariah 31
  Mary 13, 16, 25, 30, 31, 39, 41
  Merrim 41
  Nancey 26
  Nancy 31
  Robert 49, 51
  Ruth 25
  Samuel 16
  Sarah 16
  Sophia 19
  William 13, 16, 19, 25, 30, 31, 39, 41
  William Jr. 41
CLARKE, Pamelia 47

COALEY, Mary 12
  Richard 12
COCKEY, Caleb 20
  Lewis 20
  Sarah 20
COEN, Elisabeth 31
  Leonard 31
  Mary 31
  Rachel 1
COLE, 52
  Elisabeth 20
  Jonathan 20
  Mary 20
COLEMAN, Charles 2
  Charles Ridgely 9
  Curthbert William 9
  George 14
  Jane 46
  John 9
  Lydia (FORWOOD) 2
  Margaret 14
  Patren 46
  Pleasance 9, 47
  Pleasure 46
  Rebecca R. 7, 9
  Samuel Jarratt 9
  Samuel Williamson 9
  Susanna Bull 46
COLEY, Charlotte 25
  John 25
  Sarah 25
COLLET, Aaron 12
  Abraham 12
  Ann 34
  Hannah 12
  Jimmima 15
  John 29
  Matilda 15
  Moses 15, 29, 34
  Polley 15
  Rachel 15, 29, 34
  Susanna 29
COLLINS, Ann 29
  Caty Maria 28
  George 2, 28
  James 29
  John 29
  Sarah 3, 28
  Sarah (BAYLEY) 2
CONDEN, Mary 1
CONDON, Ann 1
  Hester 4
CONN, Ann 3
  Jane 3
CONNOLLY, Elisabeth 4

COOLEY, Charlotte 24
  John 24
  Mehaly 10
  Rachel 10
  Richard 10
  Sarah 24
COOP, Hannah 9
  James 9
  William 9
COOPER, Ann 20
  Catharine 20
  Eleanor 20
  Elisabeth 31
  Elizabeth 20
  Hester 20
  James 31, 42
  John Gorsuch 20
  Joseph 45
  Margaret 45
  Mary 20, 42
  Nancy 42
  Rachel 31
  Sarah 4, 20
  Sophia 45
  Thomas 20
CORBAN, Abraham 19
  Nathan 19
  Sarah 19
CORBET, Samuel 10
CORBIN, Abraham 14
  Nancy (TURNER) 2
  Nathan 14
  Rachel 14
  Temperance 2
  Thomas 2
CORBITT, Jesse 12
  John 12
  Robert 12
CORD, Elizabeth 3
COSEY, Leonard 19
  Letty 19
COURSEY, Leonard 30
  Mary 30
COWAN, Mary 4
COWELY, Abraham 27
COWEN, Leonard 2
  Mary (FOWLER) 2
COWIN, Edward 17
  Hugh 17
  Rosanna 17
  Sarah 17
COWLEY, Eleanor 18
  Margaret 18, 27
  Matthew 18, 27
  Milcah 22

COWLEY, Sarah 22
  Thomas 22
COX, 55
COYIN, Edward 20
  Elisabeth 20
CRADOCK, Elisabeth 7
CRAG, Nancy 19
  Samuel 19
  William 19
CRAGE, Ann 39
  Lovey 39
  Samuel 39
CRAIGG, Margaret 40
  Nancy 40
  Samuel 40
CRAITON, Letitia Richardson 18
  Mary 18
  Robert 18
CRAVEN, Charlotte 7
CRAWFORD, Alexander 10
  Ann 39
  Frances 10
  George 10
  Margaret 10
  Robert 39
  Sarah 39
  William 10
CRAWS, Michael 1
  Sarah (HANSON) 1
CRISMAN, Ruth 6
CRISTMAN, Frederick 52
CROMWELL, 49
  Ann 13, 14
  Elisabeth 38
  Elisabeth Ann 42
  Elizabeth Todd 14
  Henrietta 13
  John 1
  Mary 38, 39, 42
  Mary (OWINGS) 6
  Richard 6, 38
  Richard Arthur 39
  Stephen 39, 42
  Thomas 13, 14
  Urath (OWINGS) 1
CROOKS, Alexander 17
  Ann 17
  Cassandra 17
CROUCH, Elizabeth (MCGOWAN) 2
  Thomas 2
CROXALL, Eleanor 54
  Ellinor 53
  John 53, 54
CRUDGINTON, Ann 13
  George 13

CULLAM, Ann 27
  Harriott 27
  Jeremiah 27
  John Wilks Howland 27
  Margaret 27
CUNNINGHAM, Anna (AMOSS) 5
  Cassandra (LUCK) 6
  Daniel 5
  George 21, 26
  Kizziah 21, 26
  Mary 21
  Walter 6
CURRIN, Edward Fugate 42
  Sarah 42
  William 42
CURRY, Mary 3
CURRYER, Rachel 46
  Sarah 46
  William 46
CURTIS, Ann 25, 28, 34, 38, 41,
    45, 48
  Daniel 50
  Eli 45
  Eliza 48
  Ira 48
  John 50
  John Shephard 28
  Joseph 14, 38
  Levi 38
  Mary 14, 38
  Rachel 25
  Sarah 14, 41
  Thomas 34
  William 25, 28, 34, 38, 41, 45,
    48
DAILY, Elisabeth 44, 46
  Rachel 44
  Thomas 44, 46
DALL, James 4
  Sarah Brooke (HOLLIDAY) 4
DALLAS, Catharine 30
  Catharine Reed 30
  Walter 30
DARLEY, Elisabeth 34
  Harriet 34
  John Barry 34
DAVIES, Charles 28
  Elihu 28
  Elisabeth 29
  George 29
  Hannah 28
  Rebecca 1
  William 29
DAVIS, Sarah 49
DAWNEY, Sarah 7

DAWS, Ann (GRUNDEN) 4
  Edward 4
DAWSON, Isaac 29
  Mary 1
  Sarah 29
  William 29
DAY, 51
  Cassandra Fulton 21
  Charlotte E. 5
  Edward 17, 21
  Ishmael 21
  John 24
  Joshua 7
  Juliet 17
  Latitia 21
  Margaret 1
  Mary 17, 21
  Pamella 21
  Samuel 52
  Sarah (DAWNEY) 7
  William Fell 21
  Young 24
DEBRULER, Aminta (NUTTERWELL) 2
  George 2
DELANY, Ann 2
DELEVET, Ann (JONES) 4
  Peter 4
DEMOS, David 47
  Mary 47
  Susanna 47
  William 47
DEMOSS, Aquila 20
  Catharine 7
  Elijah Rutledge 27
  Jimmima 20
  John 20, 27, 37, 54
  Mary 20, 27, 37, 45
  Ruth 37
  Sarah (RANDALL) 7
  Susanna 27
  Thomas 7
  William 45
DENEATH, James 13
  Jane 13
  Samuel 13
DENISON, Matthew 5
  Sarah (SHEARWOOD) 5
DEVER, Hugh 50
DICKENS, Francis 20
  Hannah 20
  Margaret 20
DILLON, Andrew 12
  Elizabeth 12
  Mary 12
DIMMET, Dorothea 17

DIMMET, Jacob 17
  William 17
DIMMIT, William 54
DIMMITT, Nancy (TRAPNALL) 5
  William 5
DINES, Elisabeth 29
  Francis 29
  John 29
  Lovy 29
  Sarah 29
  William 29
DISNEY, Rachel 30
  Solomon 30
  William 30
DIVERS, Ababuas 24
  Ananias 28
  Ann 24
  Arranis 20
  Cassandra 6, 20, 24, 28
  Elisabeth 20
  Mary Galloway 28
  Priscilla Galloway 20
DIVES, Ananias 12
  Cassandra 12
  Salathiel Galloway 12
  Sarah 12
DIZNEY, Dinah 22
  Nancy 22
  Solomon 22
DONAVAN, Hannah 13
  Joseph 13
  William 13
DONNELL, Margaret (BRYCE) 4
  Patrick 4
DONOVAN, Charlotte (TAYLOR) 2
  Ephraim 2
  Hannah 16
  Joseph 16
  Thomas 16
DORSEY, Edward 36
  Elisabeth (SMITHSON) 4
  Henry 4
  Leven L. 36
  Patience L. 36
  Sarah (WORTHINGTON) 7
  Susan 36
  Thomas B. 7
DOWNS, Benjamin 1
  Blanch (HAMPTON) 1
  Delea 16
  Deleah (ENLOWS) 2
  Deley 24
  Henry 2, 12, 16, 24
  Jesse 14
  Mary 16

DOWNS, Samuel 12, 14, 24
  Sarah 12, 14
DOWNY, Rachel (SOTHERLAND) 6
  Robert 6
DUKE, Hester (CONDON) 4
  William 4
DULEY, Charlotte 42
  Elisabeth 42
  Thomas 42
DULY, James 29
  Martha 29
  Salley 29
DUN, Ann 36
  James 36
  Robert 36
DUNNOCK, Catharine 12
  John 12
  Thomas 12
DUNNUCK, Catharine 22, 32
  Hellen 42
  Jemima 38
  John 22, 32, 38, 42
  John Jr. 32
  Joseph Sutton 32
  Luk Wiley 38
  Rachel 22
  Sarah 32, 38, 42
DUNSTON, Ann (LIGET) 1
  Thomas 1
DURBAN, Nancy 3
DURHAM, Aquilla 51
  Lucinda (HUSBAND) 3
  Rachel (SHOUDY) 2
  Thomas 2, 50
  Zacharias 3
DWINS, Sarah 3
DYNES, Eleanor 1
EATON, Alee 23
  David 23
  John 23
  Joseph 23
  Samuel 23
  Sarah 23
EINDON, Joshua 20
ELDER, Charles 33
  Sally 33
  Violetta Elisabeth 33
ELENOS, Joshua 51
  Solomon 51
ELIOTT, Edward 10, 16
  Eleanor 10, 16
  Samuel 10, 16
  Sarah 10
  Susanna 16
  Thomas 16

ELIOTT, William 10
ELKINS, Margaretha 6
ELLENDER, Elisabeth 32
  George 3, 22, 28, 32
  Joshua 28
  Nicky Grimes 22
  Sarah 22, 28
  Sarah (GRIMES) 3
  Sary 32
ELLENOR, Barbara (BEMER) 4
  William 4
ELLIOT, Jamima 6
ELLIOTT, 55
  Abraham 18, 46, 47, 48
  Alice 40, 43, 45, 47
  Ann 21
  Ariel 46
  Arthur 21
  Benjamin 40, 43, 45, 47
  Catharine 42
  Delilah Crayton 47
  Elisabeth 45
  George 18, 44
  James 13
  James Rampley 47
  Jamima 44, 46, 47
  Jermima 43
  John 53
  John Taylor 21
  Kezia 43
  Kizziah 18
  Leonard 43, 44, 46, 47
  Margaret 21, 46, 47, 48
  Maria 46
  Mary 7, 13, 43
  Mary Jane 48
  Rachel 21, 24, 42
  Ruth Gott 40
  Sarah 24
  Sarah G. 44
  Sarah White 47
  Thomas 42
  William 21, 24
ELSROODS, Apalinia 38
  Dorcas 38
  Frederick 38
ELSROOT, Apalona 34
  Frederick 34
  Michael Gall 34
ELSWOOD, Abololey 21
  Fridrick 21
  John Frederick 21
ELY, Thomas 7
ENLOES, Henry 13
  James 15

ENLOES, James Marsh 15
  Mary 13
  Prudence 15
  Rebecca 13
ENLOWS, Deleah 2
  Henry 2
  Nancy (SAMPSON) 2
ENSON, Abraham 14
  B. 14
  William 14
ENSOR, Abraham 27
  Jane 15
  Mary 27
  Methia 27
EVERIT, Sarah (COOPER) 4
  William 4
EVERITT, Ann 27
  James 27
  William 27
EWING, Elisabeth (NORRINGTON) 7
  William 7
FATE, Elisabeth 39
  Margaret 39
FELL, Eleanor 21
  James 21
  Polly 21
FERRELL, Ruth (GALLOWAY) 4
  Thomas 4
FIFE, Grace 24
  James 24
  John 24
FINNAGAN, Aranca (SLEMAKER) 3
  Henry Patrick 3
FITZHUGH, Ann Lee 7, 16
  Daniel 8
  Daniel Dulany 48
  G. 49
  G. F. 53
  George 8, 14, 16, 51
  George Jr. 8
  Grafton Delany 14
  Henry Maynadier 48
  Margaret Murray 48
  Mary 8, 14, 16
  Walter 53
  Washington 14
FITZPATRICK, Nathan 26
  Priscilla 26
FLAHERTY, Joshua 51
FLANAGAN, Edward 19
  Elisabeth 19
  Maria 19
  Sophia 19
  Wiliam Sligh 19
FLANNAGAN, Achsah Holliday 28

FLANNAGAN, Edward 28, 51
  Elisabeth 28
  John Holliday 28
FLEAHARTY, Joshua 39
  Mary 39
  Sarah 39
FLETCHER, Catharine 21
  Elisabeth 21
  Henry 21
  James 21
  Jane 6
  John 21
  Lydia 21
  William 21
  Zachariah 21
FLEURY, Clara (YOUNG) 4
  Paul Airnee 4
FLINCHAM, Edward 20, 49
  Mary 20
  Sarah 20, 49
  Sary 49
FLOWERS, David 39
  Isabella 16
  James 39
  Jane 16
  John 16
  Mary 39
  Rachel 16
FONDY, Abraham 35
  Margaret 35
  Mary 35
FORD, Anna 6
  Catharine 38
  Joseph 11
  Lucy (JAMES) 1
  Mary 3, 11
  Thomas 38
  William 1
FORWOOD, 50
  Ann 30
  Lydia 2
  Samuel 30
  Sarah 30
FOSETT, Henry 12
  John 12
  Margaret 18
  Mary 18
FOSTER, Aaron 35
  Catharine 35
  Faithful 17
  Jesse 17
  John 35
  Mary 17
FOWLER, Ann 23, 30
  Harriot 23

FOWLER, James 30
  John 21, 23, 30
  Mary 2, 15, 30
  Nancy 21
  Reuben 21
  Richard 15, 30
  Ruth 30
  Susanna 15
FRANCIS, Ann 21, 22
  Charles 22
  Samuel 21, 22
  Sarah 21
  William 22
FRANKLIN, Benjamin 50
  James 50
  Thomas 50
FRAZER, Mary 28
  Penelope 28
  Samuel 28
  William 28
FREELAND, Aaron 45
  Abraham 22, 45
  Ann 22
  Becky 10
  Dorcas 12
  Elisabeth 22
  John 45
  Mary 22, 45
  Miranda 45
  Moses 10, 12, 22
  Naomi 10
  Rachel 12
  Rebecca 22
  Sarah 45
FROST, John 11
  Joseph 11
  Sarah 11
FUGATE, 50
  Edward 16
  Forest 19
  Martin 16, 19
  Mary 5, 16, 19
  Temperance 3
FULKS, Jacob 3
  Priscilla (PURKINS) 3
FULLER, Elisabeth 21, 39
  Elizabeth 17
  Hannah 39
  Jemmima 17
  John 21, 39
  John Hutchings 39
  Joshua K. 42
  Nancy 34
  Nicholas 17
  Samuel 21

FULLER, Sarah 34, 39
  William 34, 39
FULLERTON, James 2
  Sarah (BRADFORD) 2
FULTON, Hannah 54
  Hannah (AMOS) 7
  James 7
  Priscilla 54
  Rachel 7
GAFFORD, Aley 5
GALLION, Mary 5
GALLOWAY, Absalom 26
  Ann 31
  Ann (BARTON) 3
  Aquila 3
  Aquila Carrol 48
  Elisha 48
  Elisabeth 26
  James 2
  Jehu 14
  Jemmima 7
  Joshua 14
  Mary (CHINE) 2
  Methia 26
  Parmela 12
  Priscilla 31
  Rebecca 26
  Ruth 4
  Sarah 7, 8
  Thomas 12
  William 31, 48
GALOWAY, Mary 4
GARMAIN, Benjamin 31
  Job 31
  Rachel 31
GARRETT, Alexander 24
  Martha 24
  Rosanna 24
GARRISON, Ann 8
  Cornelius 8, 11
  John 11
  Mary (GALLION) 5
  Ruthan 5
  Sarah 8
  Susanna 8, 11
GASH, Elizabeth 16
  Michael Ashford 16
  Thomas 16
GAWTHOUP, Asenath 15
  Mary 15
  Richard 15
GAWTHROUP, Mary 20
  Richard 20
  Thomas 20
GEORGE, Sarah 2

GERMAN, John 21
  Margaret 10
  Mary 21
  Thomas 21
  Walter Presbury 10
GEST, Susanna 52
GIBSON, Eliza (BOND) 2
  Thomas 2
GILBERT, Elisabeth 7, 24, 25
  Martha (MCCOMAS) 5
  Michael 24, 25 ·
  Parker 5
GILES, Ann 4
GILLAM, Louis 2
  Temperance (CORBIN) 2
GIST, Federal Ann Buoneparte 34
  Joshua 34
GITTING, Archibald B. 39
  Elijah Bosley 39
  Elisabeth 39
GITTINGS, Ann 35
  Archibald 6, 35, 46, 53
  Eleanor Croxall 40
  Elisabeth 35, 46
  Elisabeth (BOSLEY) 6
  Eliza Ann 7
  Elizabeth 3
  George 54
  Harriett 34
  James 34, 53
  James Jr. 51
  John Sterrett 34
  Mary 1, 40
  Mary (WILMOT) 6
  Nicholas Bosley 46
  Susanna 3
  Thomas 6, 40, 54
GIVEN, Elisabeth 27
  Elisabeth (GREEN) 4
  James 4, 27
  Margaret 6
  Rachel 27
GLADDEN, Ann 10
  Barnet 10
  Elisabeth 35, 39
  Frederick 27
  H. 47
  Hannah 39, 40, 45
  Jacob 10, 27, 35, 40
  James 10
  John 10, 35, 47
  Mary 10, 27
  Sarah 35
  William 35, 39, 40, 45, 47
GLADEN, Hannah 27

GLADEN, Jacob 27
  Jane 27
  Mary 27
  William 27
GLADIN, Hannah 35
  Mary 35
  William 35
GLADMAN, Ann 35
  Michael 35
  Rebecca 35
GODMAN, Deliah (WHITE) 5
  William 5
GOE, Cassandra (JONES) 2
  Henry Bateman 3
  Susanna (GITTINGS) 3
  William 2
GOODWIN, Abby 10, 11
  Achsah 14
  Benjamin 11
  Charles Ridgely 11
  Elizabeth 10
  Henry 11
  James 13
  Lionel Lyde 11
  Lyde 10, 11
  Milcah 14
  Moses 13
  Pleasance 11
  Thomas Parkin 10
  William 14
GORDEN, Margaret 2
GORDON, Aaron 9, 21
  Elisabeth 21
  Elizabeth 9, 16
  Rebecca 21
  Ruth Gott 16
  William 16
GORSUCH, 51
  Belinda 34
  Charles 14, 17, 32
  Deborah 14
  Deley 17
  Delia 32
  Dickerson 34
  Dickinson 4, 31, 39, 43, 45
  Eleanor 43
  Elisabeth 22, 31, 37
  Elizabeth 43
  James 37
  Jesse 31
  John 51
  Kirenhappuck 32
  Keturah 27
  Lovelace 31
  Loveless 37, 43

68

GORSUCH, Lovlis 22
  Mary 31, 34, 39, 43, 45
  Mary (TALBOTT) 4
  Nathan 31
  Nicholas 43
  Nicholas Norman 27
  Norman 27
  Rachel 14, 37
  Thomas Talbott 39
  William 17, 22
GOTT, Richard 5
  Ruth (BAILEY) 5
GOVER, Elisabeth 3
  Elisabeth (GOVER) 3
  Ephraim Gittings 3
GRAFTON, Martha 11
  Nathaniel 11
  Sarah 11
GRAHAME, 51
GRANT, Catharine (HOLLAND) 2
  William 2
GRAY, Elisabeth 21
  Hannah 1
  Richard 21
GRAYHAM, Catharine 34
  Elisabeth 34
  George 34
  Hannah 34
  John 1
  Mary (MCGAWLEY) 1
  Sarah 34
GREEN, Ann 2
  Benjamin 16
  Cassandra 16, 27
  Cassandra (SMITHSON) 1
  Charles 10
  Elisabeth 4
  Harry 51
  Isaac 10
  John 1, 16, 27
  Joshua 52
  Mary Ann 27
  Matilda 26
  Rachel 26
  Rebecca 10
  Shadrack 26
  Thomas Smithson 27
GREENFIELD, Elizabeth 14
  Martha 5
  Mary 14
  Sarah 14
  William 14
GREER, Aquila 19
  James 19
  Mary 19

GREER, William 19
GREGORY, Elisabeth 28, 33
  Elizabeth 16
  George Washington 16
  John 16, 28, 33
  John N. Grimes 33
GRIFFEE, Margaret 13
  Philip 13
  Rachel 13
GRIFFIN, 52
  Amelia (MAGNESS) 7
  Ann 20
  Elizabeth 17
  James 28
  John 20, 50
  Joseph 28
  Lynch 28
  Martha 17
  Philip 28
  Rachel 28
  Rebecca 20
  Ruth 28
  Thomas 17
  William 7
GRIMES, Elisabeth 22
  Elizabeth 2
  John 22
  Polley 22
  Sarah 3
GRINDALL, Elisabeth Ann 31
  Eliza Helen 31
  Joseph 31
GROOMBRIDGE, James 52
GROVER, Charles 26
  Jamima 2
  Martha 41
  Martha Prigg 41
  Robert 41
  William 26
GROVES, Martha 4
GRUNDEN, Ann 4
GUDGEON, Elizabeth 3
GUISHARD, David 30
  Rachel 30
  Sarah 30
GUITON, Abraham 9, 13
  Ann 9, 13
  Joseph 13
  Joshua 9
GUYTON, Abraham 10, 50
  Ann 8, 10
  Benjamin 13
  Eleanor 19, 27
  Elisabeth 29, 41
  Elizabeth 1

GUYTON, Frances 13, 19, 38
Isaac 2, 10
James 27, 29
Jesse 38
John 13, 19, 27, 29
John Holt 1
Joshua 13, 27, 32, 37, 41
Margaret 13, 27, 32, 37, 41
Margaret (HETHORN) 2
Martha 27
Ruth 5
Sarah 13
Sarah (WATKINS) 1
Saray 27
William 10
GWYNN, Eleanor (CAMPBELL) 1
Elizabeth 5
Elizabeth (GWYNN) 5
Robert 5
Samuel 55
William 1
HAIR, Francis 34
Mary 34
Sarah 1
Susanna 34
HALEY, Sarah 5
HALL, Ann 24, 29, 31
Aquila 24, 29, 31, 49, 51
Charity 27
Deliah 6
Edward Carvill 31
Elisabeth (CONNOLLY) 4
Elisabeth Ann 27
Jacob 9, 26
James 4
Jane 7
John 54
Mary 9, 26
Thomas Parry 9
William 27
William Henry 24
HAMBLETON, Aley (GAFFORD) 5
Edward 7
Elizabeth 3
James 37
Jane 37
John 2, 4, 5, 37
Peggy (BOND) 4
Phebe (MAXWELL) 2
Priscilla (JOHNSON) 7
William 37
HAMILTON, Elizabeth 16
John 16, 44
Phobe 16
Phobe Maxwell 16

HAMILTON, Rebecca 16
Rosetta 44
Thomas 44
William 16
HAMMOND, Abraham 10
James Dickinson 10
Mary 10
HAMPTON, Blanch 1
HANSON, Sarah 1
HARDCASTLE, Elizabeth 1
HARE, Francis 4, 28
John 28, 51
Mary 28
Mary (GALOWAY) 4
HARP, Frederick 35
James 35
Mary 35
HARPER, Clemency 36
Elisabeth 23
Harriot 29
John 23
Joshua 36
Martha 10, 23, 29, 36
Nancy 10
Samuel 10, 23, 29, 36
HARRIS, Elizabeth 2
HARRITT, Henry 30
Jane 30
Richard 30
Sarah 30
HART, Joseph 11
Mary 22, 42
Priscilla 11
Sarah 11
William 22, 42
HARTLEY, Ezekiel 22
Leah 22, 51
Mary 22
Thomas 22
HARVEY, Elizabeth 19
James 19
William 19
HARWOOD, John 22
Margaret 22
Walter 22
HASP, Frederick 35
James 35
Mary 35
HATRARTY, Abraham 18
Ann 18
Joshua 18
HAYES, Ann 16, 38
Cassandra 10, 16, 38
Elisabeth 41
Elizabeth 10, 16

HAYES, George 16
  Harriot 41
  Isaac 41
  James 10, 16, 38
  Jesse 16
  Nicholas 16
HAYS, Rebecca 2
HEALTY, George 36
  James 36
  John 36
  Sary 36
HEAP, Ann Kent 35
  Charity 35
  Elisabeth 35
  John 35
  Mary 35
  Thomas 35
  William Bankhead 35
HEAPE, Charity 24, 29
  Isabella 29
  Jesse 29
  John 24, 29
  Mary 24, 29
  Sarah 24
  Thomas 29
HENDEN, Benjamin 15
  Josias 15
  Sophia 15
HENDON, 54
  Benjamin 20
HENDRICK, Joshua 7
  Sarah (GALLOWAY) 7
HENRY, Ann (PRICE) 5
  Henry O. 5
HERINGTON, Elizabeth 14
HERRINGTON, Betsey 24
  Hannah 24
  John 24
  Sarah 24
HETHORN, Margaret 2
HICKERSON, Dorcas Baker 11
  Elizabeth 11
  Mary (THRAP) 1
  Samuel 1, 11
HICKS, 52
  Abraham 36
  Rebecca 36
  Sarah 36
HILL, Eleanor 49
  Elisabeth 36
  Flemmon 49
  Lewis 36
  Mary 36, 49
  Richard 36
  William 36

HILTON, Abraham 2, 15, 21, 22,
  26, 28, 32
  Betsey 28
  Elisabeth 21, 26, 28, 32
  Elizabeth 15
  Elizabeth (GRIMES) 2
  John 16, 22, 26, 31
  Kitura 31
  Lydia 16, 22, 31
  Nancy 15
  Patty 21
  William 32
HINDON, Mary 7
HINES, Elizabeth (LAWRENCE) 6
  William Bois 6
HIPKINS, Charles 1
  Elizabeth (MYRES) 1
HITCHCOCK, Abraham 17
  Ann 17
  Aquila Clark 17
  Asael 13, 17
  Charity 17
  Claudius 35, 48
  Easter 14
  Elisabeth 35
  Emilia 14
  Esther 17
  Isaac 17
  Israel 17
  Jemima 3
  Jesse 31, 35
  John 14, 17
  Josiah 17
  Keziah 17
  Leah 13
  Mary 31, 35
  Sarah 13, 17, 31
  Sarah Ann 48
  Susanna 17, 35, 48
  Susanna Garland 35
HOCKLEY, Elisabeth 32
  John 32
HOGGES, Allen 21
  John 21
  Rachel 21
  Samuel 21
  William 21
HOLDER, Mary 20
  Priscalla 20
HOLDING, Peter 1
  Sarah (HAIR) 1
HOLLAND, Catharine 2
  Francis 5
  Sybel (WEST) 5
HOLLIDAY, Eleanor A. 6

HOLLIDAY, Eleanor Addison 12, 52
  Elizabeth Carnan 12
  John Robert 12, 52
  Mary Lee 12
  Prudence Gough 12
  Rebecca Ridgely 12
  Sarah Brooke 4
HOLLINGSWORTH, Cassandra
  (DIVERS) 6
  Isaac 6
  Jesse 2
  Rachel Lyde (PARKIN) 2
HOLLINSHADE, John Smith 42
  Priscilla 42
  Titus 42
HOLMES, Gabriel 4, 44
  Mary 44
  Mary (BACON) 4
HOOD, Charles Crook 12
  Henrietta 36
  Margaret 12
  Thomas 12
HOOFMAN, Deborah (OWINGS) 6
  Peter 6
HOOK, Elisabeth 33
  Jacob 33
  Sarah 33
HOOPER, Asael Wilson 21
  Isaac 14, 21
  Keziah 14
  Kizziah 21
  Michael 14
HOPKINS, Ann (JENKINS) 4
  Charles 4
  Eleanor (MORGAN) 5
  Elisabeth 7
  John 5
  Joseph 6
  Sarah (MORGAN) 6
  Thomas 49
HORNER, Delia (CARROLL) 6
  Nathan 6
HOWARD, Alce 24
  Ann 11
  Aquila 50
  Blanch 52
  Charlotte (RUMSEY) 5
  Edward Aquila 5
  Elisabeth 4, 30
  Eliza August 29
  Frances Cordelia 29
  George 30
  Grace 24
  Henry 24
  John 30

HOWARD, John Beale 54
  Lemuel 11
  Margart 30
  Martha 11
  Martha S. 43
  Martha Susanne (TALLY) 4
  Nancey 50
  Sarah 4
  Susanna 43
  T. Gazaway 54
  Thomas G. 43, 53
  Thomas Gassaway 4, 29
HOWLAND, Ann 32
  John 32
  Mary 32
HUDSON, Daniel 54
  Dorothea (BATTEN) 1
  James 1
  Susanna 52
HUGHES, Ann Bull 38
  Aquila 44
  Benjamin 50
  Elisabeth 24, 28, 35
  Elizabeth (GUDGEON) 3
  Frances 21
  Hannah 5, 6, 24
  Horatio 49
  James 21
  Jemimah 42
  John 3
  John Taylor 24
  Joshua 38
  Luther 43
  Rachel 38, 41, 43, 44, 46
  Samuel 35, 38, 41, 42, 43, 44, 46
  Sarah 35, 38, 42
  Taylor 24
  Vincent 41
  William 28
  William Plummer 28
HUGHS, Frances 3
  James 9
  Margaret 9
HULET, Catharine 20
  James 20
  Matthew 20
HULSE, Eliza 54
HUNT, Ann 1, 9
  Elisabeth 23
  Elizabeth 14
  George 14
  Mary 9
  Ruth 23
  Thomas 9

HUNT, William 14, 23
HUNTER, 50
 Betsey 42
 Bettcey 47
 Elizabeth 9
 James 5
 Jemima (INLOES) 5
 Joseph 9
 Nancy 3
 Peter G. 47
 Peter Grubb 47
 Pleasant 47
 Ralph 42
 William 42
HUSBAND, Lucinda 3
HUSBANDS, Elisabeth 5
 Susanna 2
HUTCHINGS, 55
 Ann 18, 33
 Ariel 33
 Catharine 11
 Delea 7, 8
 Edward 32
 Eleanor 11, 32
 Elisabeth 6, 46
 Elizabeth 11, 14, 18
 Ellen Maria 43
 Ellenider 43
 Ellinder 43
 Hannah 6, 11
 James 6
 Jamima 45
 Jemima 12, 32, 33, 43
 Jemmima 14, 19
 Jemmima (GALLOWAY) 7
 Jesse 7, 43, 45
 John 32, 43, 45
 Joshua 11, 12, 14, 18, 19, 28,
  33, 43, 55
 Margaret 11
 Margaret (GIVEN) 6
 Mary 18
 Matilda 8
 Menander 13
 Nicholas 13, 18, 29, 43
 Richard 19
 S. 29
 Salley 12
 Samuel 18
 Sarah 18, 29
 Susanna 11, 54
 Thomas 18, 32, 45
 William 11, 28, 32, 43, 46
 William H. 45
HUTCHINS, Ann 44

HUTCHINS, Elisabeth 44
 Elizabeth 4
 Ellen Maria 44
 Frances 26
 Jamima 44
 Jemima 26, 48
 Jesse 44
 John 47
 Joshua 26
 Joshua Lynch 48
 Lovisah 48
 Mary 44, 45
 Matilda 44
 Nicholas 47
 Richard 48
 Sarah 3, 7, 45, 48
 Thomas 48
 Thomas F. 44
 William 44, 45, 47
 Zany Ann 44
HYOT, Susanna 33
 William 33
INGLE, Dorcas 28
 William 28
INGRAM, Charles Edward Ridgely
  41
 Charles G. Ridgely 41
 Ruth 41
INLOES, Jemima 5
INLOWS, Mary 2
IRWIN, Anna 20
 Effee 20
 John 20
 Margaret 20
ISGRIGG, Ann 18, 29
 Robert 18
 Thomas 29
 William 18, 29
JACKSON, Anna Maria 43
 Edward 39
 Elisabeth 21, 23, 26, 31, 39,
  41, 43
 Elizabeth 30, 53
 Harriott 31
 John 21, 23, 26, 31, 39, 41, 43
 Juliet 26
 Martha 41
 Mary (BLAYDON) 6
 Sarah 21
 Thomas 30
 William 6, 30
JAMES, Ann 31
 Eliakim 33, 37, 53
 Elisabeth 31
 Elisabeth (SHEARWOOD) 5

73

JAMES, Frances 31
  Joseph 5
  Juliana 37
  Leah 16
  Lucy 1
  Parmelia 33, 37
  Sarah 16
  Susanna 16, 22
  William 16, 22, 33
JARMAN, Rachel 26
  Sarah 26
  William 26
JARVIS, Widow 52
JENKINS, Ann 4
  Henry 23
  Mary 12
  Oswald 6
  Samuel 12
  Sarah (PEARCE) 6
  Temperance 23
  Thomas Smith 12
JENKINSON, Ann 16
  Isabella 16
  Robert 16
  William 16
JINKINS, Ann 9
  Robert 9
  Sarah 9
JOHNS, (Mrs.) 49
  Henry 17
  Henry Hosier 17
  Hosea 4
  Penelope (SLADE) 4
  Sarah 17
  Susanna 6
JOHNSON, 53, 54
  Abraham 11
  Ann 5, 6, 25, 29, 31, 34, 35,
    36, 40, 41, 42, 43, 53
  Ann (GILES) 4
  Barnet 11, 13, 22, 25, 29, 31,
    34, 39
  Benjamin 32
  Charles 5, 35
  David 25, 32, 34, 52
  Edward 35
  Eleanor 6, 11, 29
  Eleanor (JOHNSON) 6
  Eleanor Caroline 36
  Elisabeth 5, 32, 40, 44
  Elisabeth (CRADOCK) 7
  Elisabeth (TAYLOR) 5
  Elisabeth Sollers 29
  Elisha 32
  Elisha Sollers 29

JOHNSON, Elizabeth 4
  Elizabeth (CORD) 3
  Ellenor 34
  Fayette 7, 44
  George 9
  George William 29
  Hickman 29, 36, 42
  Hithe Hickman 42
  James 29, 35
  Jane 25, 29, 31, 34, 39
  Jeremiah 29
  John 25
  Joshua 9
  Josias 3
  Loyd 43
  M. 48
  Margaret 31
  Mary 11, 32
  Mary (FUGATE) 5
  Mary Ann 40
  Moses 51
  Peggy (MORGAN) 3
  Priscilla 7
  Rachel 11, 13, 22
  Rhoda 13
  Richard 6
  Robert 31, 40
  Ruth 11
  Sarah 2, 11, 22, 32, 34
  Thomas 3, 4, 5, 13, 25, 29, 31,
    32, 35, 40, 41, 52
  Unity 9
  William 11, 43
JOLLEY, Cassandra 4
JOLLY, Elizabeth 49
JONES, Abraham 1
  Ann 4, 13
  Archibald 31
  Benjamin 1
  Cassandra 2
  Charles 35, 39, 41
  Cordelia (BAKER) 5
  Elisabeth 35, 41
  Elisabeth Robinson 35
  Henry 13
  John 41
  Magdaline 1
  Mary 39
  Mary (GITTINGS) 1
  Morgan 5
  Priscilla 39
  Richard 50
  Sarah 1, 13, 31
  Sarah (JONES) 1
  Stephen 39

JONES, Thomas Johnson 31
  William 31
JORDAN, Eleanor 39
  John 7
  Mary 39, 46
  Rachel (FULTON) 7
  Thomas 39
JORDON, Ann 17
  Eleaner 17
  Sarah 17
  William 17
JUEL, Magdalane 3
KEATH, Delila 45
  John 45
KEETH, Ann Hart 32
  John 32
  Magdalene 32
  Sarah 12
  William 12
KEITH, 52
KELL, Eleanor 19
  Flemmon 19
  Francis 19
KELLEY, Cassandra 25
  James 10
  Lurana 10
  Thomas 25
  Unity 10
  William 25
KELLY, Deliah (POCOCK) 2
  Edward 2
KELSEY, Jamima Hutchins 48
  Joshua 48
  Sarah 48
KELSO, Elijah Rutledge 18
  Elisabeth 40
  James 26, 40
  Jane 21
  John 26
  Joshua 7
  Penelope 18, 26
  Sarah (HUTCHINS) 7
  Thomas 18, 21
  William 40
KELSOE, Joshua 11
  William 11
KEMPE, Hannah 50
KENARD, Howard 41
  Mary 41
  Matthew 41
KENT, Jesse 24
  Nancy 24
  Rachel 24
KERNS, James 43
  John 7, 43

KERNS, Mary (ELLIOTT) 7
KEY, Alkee 17
  Charity 2
  James 17
  John McDaniel 17
KIDD, James 25, 36
  Joshua Hardesty 25
  Letitia 36
  Penelope 25
  Pensely 36
  Rhoda 25
KILSO, Ariel Hutchins 47
  Joshua 47
  Sarah 47
KIMBOLEY, Bond James 1
  Mary Mills (MILLS) 1
KINZIL, Ann (JOHNSON) 5
  Charles 5
KNIGHT, Ann 8
LAMBDAN, Catharine 29
  George 29
  John 29
  Thomas 29
LAMBDEN, Catharine 43
  Elijah 43
  Kitty 43
  Thomas 43
LANCASTER, Ann Maria 7
LAURENCE, John 5
  Rebecca (YARLEY) 5
LAWRENCE, Elizabeth 6
LAY, Penelope D. 20
  Robert 20
  Temprance 20
LEACH, Ann 13
  Benjamin 13, 22
  Elisabeth 22
  Elizabeth 55
  John 26
  Mary 13, 26
  Nephel 22
  Sarah 13, 22
LEADLEY, Isaac 4
  Nancey (MACKUBBINS) 4
LEAFE, John 33
  Rachel 33
  Rebecca 33
LEE, Absalom 11
  Anna 39
  Blanch 2
  Blanch Hall 17
  Caleb 11
  Edward 39, 46
  Elisabeth 9
  Elisabeth (SMITHSON) 7

LEE, Elizabeth 17
  Hugh Whiteford 46
  James 9
  John 9
  Margaret (DAY) 1
  Martha 9
  Mary 1
  Parker 9
  Parker Hall 17
  Ralph 7
  Robert 11
  Sarah Chew 5
  Susanna 39, 46
  William 1
  William Dellam 9
LEEDEN, James 14
  Mary 14
  Ruth 14
LEGE, Mary 16
  Nathan 16
LEGET, Jessee 10
  Milor 10
LERTCH, Sarah 3
LESOURD, Daniel 13
  John 13
  Mary 13
  Peter 13
LEWIS, Mary 3
LIDDON, George 19
  Mary 19
  William 19
LIGET, Ann 1
LIGHTFOOT, Alice 22
  Elisabeth 22
  John 22
LINHAM, Sarah (PINIX) 5
  William 5
LITTLE, Elisabeth 41
  Elisabeth (ADAMS) 4
  John 4, 41
  William 41
LOGAN, Alexander 25
  James 25
  Jane 25
  Joseph 25
  Mary 25
LONDERSLAGER, Anne 36
  Cecelia 36
  Elisabeth 35
  Francis 35
  Jacob 35
  Mary 35
  Solomon 36
LONG, Aquila 33
  Eliza Ann (GITTINGS) 7

LONG, Elizabeth 33
  Henry 7
  James 27
  Margaret 23, 27
  Margaret (CARR) 2
  Nancey 23
  Peter 2, 23, 27
LONGDAN, Arthur 3
  Mary (LEWIS) 3
LORNQUIS, George 6
  Margaretha (ELKINS) 6
LOVE, Bennet 7
  Elisabeth (GILBERT) 7
  John 49, 53
  Robert 53
LOW, Isaac 3
  Jemima (HITCHCOCK) 3
LUCAS, John 3
  Sarah (DWINS) 3
LUCK, Cassandra 6
  Catharine 20, 22
  Esau 20, 22
  George 22
  Mary 20
LUX, Darby 33, 52
  Elisabeth Ann 33
  Mary 33, 52
LYNCH, Anthony 3
  Eleanor 19
  Elisabeth 33
  Eliza 19
  Frances 19
  Kid 2
  Lawrence 19
  Mary 19
  Mary (BARTON) 3
  Patrick 33
  Sarah (SWARTH) 2
  William 33
LYTLE, Alexander Mc Comas 16
  Elisabeth 27
  Elizabeth 14, 16
  George 14, 16, 27, 51
  Nathan 27
  Thomas 14
LYTTLE, Elisabeth 33
  John 33
MACKABEE, Jamima (GROVER) 2
  William 2
MACKEY, James Howard 34
  Ruth 34
  William 34
MACKUBBINS, Nancey 4
MACORD, Arthur 45
  James 45

MACORD, Jesse 45
  Sarah 45
MAGAW, John 3
  Sarah (HUTCHINS) 3
MAGNESS, Amelia 7, 16
  James 40
  John 40
  Moses 16
  Rachel 16, 40
  Sarah (WATERS) 2
  William 2
MARCHE, Hannah (ONION) 4
  John 4
MARKEY, Marget 30
  Rebecca 30
  William 30
MARSH, Beale 44
  Charlotte 14
  Clement 6, 41
  Dennis 44
  Elijah 44
  Ellen 44
  Grafton 44
  James Elliott 41
  Jemima (ELLIOT) 6
  John 54
  Joshua 44
  Josiah 44
  Nelson 44
  Rachel 23
  Rebecca 44
  Sarah 14, 23
  Sophia 23
  Stephen 44
  Temperance 44
  Thomas 14, 23, 53
  Thomas Beale 41
MARTIN, Alexander 11
  Eleanor 11
  Henry 22
  Mary 22
  Samuel 22
  William 11
MASON, Ann 33
  Ann (CONDON) 1
  Catherine 33
  George 33
  John 1
  Michael 33
MATHERS, 50
MATTHEWS, Ann (CONN) 3
  Jesse 3
MATTOCKS, Charity 19
  Mary 19
MAULSBY, Eleanor 3

MAULSBY, Eleanor (MAULSBY) 3
  Israel D. 7, 45
  Jame (HALL) 7
  Jane 45
  John Hall 45
  Maurice 3
MAXWELL, Elizabeth (ROGERS) 6
  Moses 4
  Phebe 2
  Robert 6
  Salley Charity (BOND) 4
MCCAIRNAN, Nancy 5
MCCAUSLAND, Barbara 51
MCCLUNG, Eleanor 42
  James 42
  Mary Ann 42
MCCLURE, Elisabeth 24
  Mary 2
  Sarah 24
  William 24
MCCOLLOUGH, Elizabeth 15
  Robert 15
  Ruth 15
  William 15
MCCOMAS, 50, 54
  Aaron 44
  Alexander 11
  Amos 17
  Ann 17, 23
  Aquila 33
  Calvel 44
  Cassandra 10
  Clemency 17
  Daniel 5, 50
  Elisabeth 23
  Elisabeth (ONION) 4
  Elisabeth (SCOTT) 5
  Elizabeth 17
  Frederick 2
  James 4, 10, 17, 23, 27, 50
  James Preston 23
  John 17
  Josiah Scott 23
  Josias 23
  Martha 5, 33, 44
  Mary 17, 23
  Moses 23, 50
  Nicholas Day 4
  Preston 11
  Priscilla 10, 23, 27
  Robert Amos 33
  Sarah 17
  Sarah (HOWARD) 4
  Scott 27
  Susanna 11

MCCOMAS, Susanna (ONION) 2
MCCORMACK, George 10
  Johnson 10
MCCRACKEN, John 3
  Sarah (SMITH) 3
MCCREERY, Letecia 12
  Mary 12
  Ralph 12
MCCUBBIN, John 3
  Polley (TUDER) 3
MCCUBBINS, John 23
  Lloyd 11
  Polley 23
  Sarah 11
  Susanna 3
  Zaccariah 23
MCCULLOCK, Benjamin 17
  Robert 17
MCDONNEL, Elizabel 15
  Elizabeth 15
  John 15
  Mary 15
MCFADDEN, Ann 22
  Margaret 22
  William 22
MCFADDIN, Charles 32
  Thoma Wilson 32
  William 32
MCGAW, John 21
  Mary 21
  Richard 21
MCGAWLEY, Mary 1
MCGOVERN, Mark 11
  Mary 11
MCGOWAN, Catharine Johnson 19
  Elizabeth 2
  John 19
  Mary 19
MCLAUGHLIN, Dennis 1
  Mary (DAWSON) 1
MCLUNG, Joseph 13
  Robert 13
MCMATH, Mary 46
  Mary (CURRY) 3
  Samuel 3, 46
  Sarah (MOORES) 3
  William 3
MCNABB, Isaac 25
  Jane 25
  Sarah 25
MEADS, James 48
  John Demoss 48
  Susanna 48
MECATHEA, Jehu Galloway 14
  Joshua Galloway 14

MECATHEA, Thomas 14
MERRIMAN, Benjamin 14
  Mary 14
  Rebecca 14
MERRYMAN, 53
  Ann 40, 51
  Ann Mariah 32
  Benjamin 36, 51
  Catharine 4, 7, 18
  Charlotte (WORTHINGTON) 6
  Deborah 18, 30
  Eleaner 18
  Eleaner Cassandra 34
  Elijah 13, 52
  Elisabeth 34
  Elisabeth Johnson 23
  Elizabeth 13, 52
  Ellenor 50
  Frances 13
  Gerard 41
  John 2, 18, 23, 32, 34
  Joshua 53
  Levi 32
  Martha 40, 53
  Mary 6, 34
  Milcah 7
  Nicholas 5, 6, 18, 30, 34, 36,
    40, 41, 53
  Sarah 18, 23, 32, 34, 36, 40
  Sarah (ANDERSON) 5
  Sarah (JOHNSON) 2
  Sarah Dauvidge 52
  Sary 41
METTEE, Catharine 21, 34
  Cathrine 29
  Henry 29
  John Jacob 34
  Leonard 21, 29, 34
MIDDLETON, John 4
  Mary (COWAN) 4
MILES, Abraham 12
  Aquila 12, 24, 28, 34, 35, 39,
    54
  Caty 24
  Elisabeth 34, 35
  Elisha 34
  Elizabeth 14
  Hannah 12
  James 12
  Jane 9, 26
  John 9, 39
  Joshua 9, 26, 28
  Lewis 14
  Margaret 26, 35
  Rebecca 26

MILES, Thomas 12, 14
MILLER, Bethia 43
  Cathrenah Mary 18
  Edward 25
  Elisabeth 45
  Elizabeth 51
  Hannah 16, 30
  Henry 25, 41
  Henry Leonard 18
  Jacob Colson 25
  Jacob Coulson 25
  James 24
  Jesse 41
  John 16, 24, 43
  John Joseph 18
  John Martin 18
  Joseph 45
  Mary 24, 45
  Robert 30
  Samuel 24
  Sarah 24, 25, 41, 43
  Thomas 16, 30
MILLIKIN, Susannah 3
MILLS, Mary Mills 1
MOALE, Frances (OWINGS) 6
  Robert North 6
MONGOMERY, James 10
  Susanne 10
  Thomas 10
MONKS, Anna Bella 26
  Elicia 26
  John 26
  Louisa 26
  Mary Ann 26
  William 26
MONOHON, Arthur 16, 32
  Blanch 32
  Charlotte 32
  James 32
  Sarah 16, 32
MONTGOMERY, Abraham 24
  James 1, 24, 27, 37
  Nancy 37
  Ruth 2
  Susanna 24, 27, 37
  Susanna (WHITAKER) 1
MOOBERRY, David 34
  Elisabeth 34, 39, 43
  John 39
  Samuel 43
  William 34, 39, 43
MOOBERY, Ann 18
  Elisabeth 25
  Elizabeth 18
  Jane 18

MOOBERY, William 18, 25
MOOBURY, Alexander 29
  Elizabeth 29
  William 29
MOORE, Deliah (HALL) 6
  Gay 38
  John 5
  Mary (SCARBROUGH) 5
  Nicholas Ruxton 38
  Philip 6
  Rebecca 38
  Sarah 38
MOORES, Aquila Paca 20
  Daniel 3
  James 11
  John 1, 11, 17, 20
  Mary 11, 17, 20
  Mary (LEE) 1
  Samuel Lee 17
  Sarah 3, 50
  Sarah (BUDD) 3
MOPS, Fredrick 30
  Nancy 30
MOREN, Agnes 9
  Jenney 9
  Thomas 9
  William 9
MORFORD, Thomas G. 34
  Thomas Garrison 34
MORGAN, Cassandra Lee 5
  Edward 13, 17
  Eleanor 5
  Elisabeth 24
  Elisabeth Hawkins 24
  Elizabeth 2, 25
  Elizabeth Hawkins 25
  Martha 9, 13
  Mary 2, 9, 17
  Peggy 3
  Robert 9, 13, 24, 25
  Samuel 17
  Sarah 3, 6
  Thomas John Hamilton 9
  William 51
  William Groom 9
MORRIS,   50
  Belinda 22
  Edward 46
  Electius 42
  Jamima 42
  Jemima 46
  Lewis 46
  Rebecca 22
  Samuel 22
MULLOY, James 1

MULLOY, Sarah (WEEKS) 1
MURREY, Elizabeth 16
  Ruth 16
MURRY, Elizabeth 2
  Hannah 4
  James 4, 26
  Mary 26
  Susanna 26
  Susanne (SWANN) 4
MYERS, George 18
  Henrietta 27
  Henry 18, 27, 29
  Sarah 18, 29
MYRES, Elizabeth 1
NASH, Lucresy 14
  Lucretia (WEEKS) 1
  Thomas 1
NEAL, John 1
  Mary (SCOFIELD) 1
NEILL, Ann 5
  Mary (SHEREDINE) 5
  William 5
NELSON, Elisabeth Bower 46
  Elisabeth Boner 46
  Hannah 43, 46, 47
  Hannah (HUTCHINGS) 6
  John 46, 47
  John Hutchins 44
  Nicholas Hutchins 47
  Richard Hutchings 46
  Sarah 43, 47
  William 6, 43, 46
NEVILL, Ann 15
  John 15
  Rachel 15
  Rebecca 15
  Simon 15
NEWALL, Elizabeth Claypole 17
  James 17
  Martha 17
NICHOLAS, Elizabeth (HARRIS) 2
  Nathaniel 2
NICHOLS, Frances 3
NICHOLSON, Benjamin 26
  Charles Ridgely 8
  Eleanor 26
  J. 51
  John 51
  John Ridgely 4
  Mary 8, 26
  Matilda 51
  Matilda Heath (SMITH) 4
  Sarah 26, 51
NIGER, Michael 3
  Sarah (MORGAN) 3

NIGHT, Christopher 14
  Cloender 14
  John 14
  Susanna 14
NORRINGTON, Elisabeth 7
NORRIS, Abraham 15, 50
  Ann 27, 42, 45
  Daniel 3
  Daniel Treadaway 38
  Edward 18
  Elisabeth 34, 38, 40
  Elizabeth 15, 18
  Esrom Hughes 38
  Frances (HUGHS) 3
  George 18, 38, 40
  George Chocke 34
  Greenberry Wiley 38
  Hannah 4, 27, 45
  Henry 2
  James 27, 42
  John 27, 36, 42, 45
  John Philips 30
  Katy 46
  Margaret (GORDEN) 2
  Martha 3
  Mary 27, 30, 34, 45, 46
  Nancy 36
  Rachel 1
  Rebecca 15
  Susannah 46
  Thomas 36
  Widow 49
  William 30, 46
NORTON, John 1
  Sarah (JONES) 1
NUTTERWELL, Aminta 2
OHARROW, Ignatius 42
  Kerenhappuck 42
  Sally 42
ONION, Elisabeth 4, 28
  Hannah 4
  Rebecca Weston 28
  Susanna 2
  William 28
OSBURN, Harry Page 26
  William 26
OTHARSON, Rebecca 2
OWINGS, Ann 11
  Ann (JOHNSON) 6
  Arrianna 38
  Beal 35
  Deborah 6, 11
  Elisabeth 23
  Eliza 35
  Elizabeth 10

OWINGS, Frances 6
Julianna 38
Lucy 23
Mary 6, 11
Mary Harrowood 10
Nicholas 23
Rachel 38
Ruth 6, 34, 35
Samuel 11, 34, 38, 53
Stephen 10, 23, 50
Susanna 6
Thomas Beale 6
Urarth 1
Uriah 49
William 23
William Lynch 34
PARISH, Benjamin 3
Elizabeth (JOHNSON) 4
Nancy (HUNTER) 3
Nicholas 4
PARK, Aquila 28
Elisabeth 28
William 28
PARKER, Ann 28
Isham 28
John 28
Nicholas 47
Penelope 47
Samuel 47
PARKIN, Rachel Lyde 2
PARMER, Ann 15
Edward 38
Eleanor 30
George 30, 38
John 40
John Ellis 40
Margaret 30, 38
Mary 40
Samuel 15
Sarah 15
William 15
PATRICK, George 2
Ruth (MONTGOMERY) 2
PAUL, Elisabeth 25
Jonathan 25
Susannah 25
Waltera 54
PEAK, Catharine 30
Elisabeth 28, 30
Elizabeth (MURRY) 2
James W. 30
John 30
Robert 2, 28, 30
PEARCE, Elisabeth 40
Sarah 6

PEARCE, William 40
PERDEW, Elisabeth 30, 38
Walter 30, 38
William 30
PERDUE, Elisabeth 28, 46
John 46
Mary 28
Thomas 46
Walter 28, 46, 49
PERRY, Alice 4
Ann 9, 10
Frances 9, 10
Henry 10
John 9, 10
Samuel 9
Sarah 9
Susanna 10
William 9, 10
PHILPOT, Bryan 5, 36, 39, 42
Elisabeth 36, 39, 42
Elisabeth (JOHNSON) 5
Elisabeth Hance 42
John 39
PHIPPS, John 17, 18
Mary 18
Nathan 1
Nathaniel 17
Rebecca 17
Rebecca (DAVIES) 1
William 18
PICKET, John 45
Temperence 45
PIERCE, Elisabeth 37
John Bacon 37
Thomas 37
Thomas P. 54
PILES, Ralph 49
Samuel 49
PINIX, Sarah 5
PLOWMAN, Johathan 22
Susanna 22
POCOCK, Ann 18, 28, 34, 38
Asenath 44
Caterina 45
Catharina 45
Catharine 14, 28, 34, 36, 38,
40, 43, 44
Charity 34, 51
Daniel 18, 52
Daniel Smith 34
David 4, 27, 29, 34, 41, 44,
45, 47, 48, 52
Deliah 2
Eleanor 3, 36
Eli 28

81

POCOCK, Elijah 45
  Elizabeth Ellen 48
  Fanny 54
  Israrel 40
  James 18, 34, 38
  James Wiles 45
  Jemima 14
  Jesse 14, 28, 34, 36, 38, 40,
    43, 44, 45
  John 44
  John Thomas 45
  Juliet Elisabeth 45
  Kezia 38
  Mary 27, 29, 34, 41, 43, 44,
    45, 47, 48
  Mary (SMITH) 4
  Mary Ann 41
  Rachel Fugate 38
  Rebecca Jane 45
  Robert 29
  S. 52
  Salome 47
  Sarah 8, 18, 27
  Ustinah 45
PORDUE, Elizabeth 18
  Laban 18
  William 18
PORTER, James 31
  Robert 31
  Susanna 31
POTTEE, Sarah 4
POTTER, Cordelia 22
  Elisabeth 22, 26
  John 22, 26
  Thomas 26
PRESBURY, Mary 5
PRESTON, Anna 1
  Chloe Ady 43
  John 43
  Rachel 7
  Rebecca 43
PRICE, Ann 5
  Elisabeth 38, 42
  John 38, 42
  Joseph 38
PRIGG, Edward 17
  Elizabeth 10
  John 10, 15
  Martha 1
  Mary 10, 15
  Susanna 17, 23
  William 15, 17, 23
PRINE, Ann 13
  Benjamin 13
  John 13

PROCTON, Milly 3
PROSER, Ann 16
  Asel 16
  David 16
  Elizabeth 16
  Hannah 16
  Mary 16
PURKINS, Priscilla 3
PYLE, Ralph 53
  Sarah 54
QUARLES, Elisabeth (HUSBANDS) 5
  John 5
RAINE, Charlotte (CRAVEN) 7
  Thomas 7
RAMPLEY, Ann 41
  Charles Mayes 41
  Christana 46
  Christian 47
  Christiana 36, 41
  Elisabeth 41
  James 9, 41
  Jamima 47
  Mary 36
  Patty Mayes 41
  Phillemon 41
  Sarah 9, 47
  Sary 46
  Susanna Mayes 41
  Thomas 36, 41, 46, 47
  William 41
RAMPLY, Nancy 45
  Sarah 45
  William 45
RANDALL, Sarah 7
RANGE, Ann 35
  John 35
  Sarah 35
RAWINGS, Nathaneal R. 54
RAWLEY, Daniel 2
  Mary (ROBB) 2
READ, Agnes 33
  Hugh 33
  Joseph 33
REED, Aaron Tunis 21
  Agness 29, 42
  Ann (HUNT) 1
  Emanuel 1
  Joseph 29, 42
  Mary 29
  Rebecca 2
  Viney 21
  William 21
REES, Daniel 21
  Elisabeth 21
  Mary 21

82

RENNER, Catharine 5
RENSHAW, Ann 18
  Catharine 18
  Elizabeth 18
  Magdaline (JONES) 1
  Martin 1
  Mary 18
  Robert 18
RICHARDSON, 55
  Benjamin 15, 21
  David 42
  Eleanor 22
  James 15, 22
  Jamima 37, 42
  Jamima Ann 46
  John 15, 42
  Mary 9, 21, 37, 42, 46
  Mary (MORGAN) 2
  Penelope 31, 52
  Rebecca 22
  Ruth 9
  Samuel 42, 55
  Sarah 15, 42, 49
  Skelton Standiford 31
  Thomas 9, 21, 37, 46
  Vincent 31
  William 2, 39
  William Altee 39
RICKETS, Ann 6
RICKETTS, Hannah Rebecca 21
  Samuel 21
  Susanna 21
RIDGELEY, Ruth 54
RIGBY, Eleanor 37
  Eleanor (SMITH) 1
  George 1, 37
RIGLEY, James 17
  Margaret 17
RINGGOLD, John Galloway 37
  Mary 37
  Thomas 37
RISTEAU, Abraham 14
  Benjamin Denny 37
  Charles Walker 37
  Elisabeth 37, 40
  Elizabeth 14
  John 14
  John L. 40
  John Talbot 37
  Richard Casson 40
  Robert Carnan 37
  Thomas Cradock 37
  William McLaughlin 37
RITTER, Elisabeth 33
  Sidnay 33

RITTER, Thomas 33
ROACH, Elizabeth (HAMBLETON) 3
  William 3
ROBB, Mary 2
ROBERTS, Benjamin 22, 32
  Maria (SANDERSONS) 3
  Mary 22
  Peter John 3
  Taratius 22
  Terrecen 32
  Zachariah 32
ROBINET, Elizabeth 51
ROBINSON, Aquila 15
  Charles 15
  Margaret 49
  Mepheteka 15
  Walter 15
ROCK, Rebecca (REED) 2
  Thomas 2
ROCKHOLD, Ann Eleanor 43
  Charles 3, 8, 27, 31, 43
  Eleanor 8, 2 31, 43
  Eleanor (POCOCK) 3
  Elijah 27
  Jesse 31
  John 2
  Martha (WATERS) 2
  Sarah 34
  Thomas 34
RODES, Benjamin 10
  Elisabeth 10
  John 10
ROE, Ann 12
  Athaliah 22
  Edward 22
  Isham 22
  Joshua 22
  Mary 49
  Sarah 12
  William 12, 49
ROGERS, Catharine 52
  Elizabeth 6, 8
ROSER, Adam 35
  Elisabeth 35
  Joseph 35
  Susanna 35
ROUSE, Christopher Chapman 44
  John 44
  Sarah 44
RUFF, Anna (PRESTON) 1
  Henry 1
RUMSEY, Amelia Jane 20
  Benjamin Jr. 52
  Charles Henry 31
  Charlotte 5

RUMSEY, Hannah 20, 31
  Henry 20, 31
  Maria 20
RUSH, Arnold 3
  Jane (CONN) 3
RUTLEDGE, Abraham 14
  Ann (BURTON) 4
  Augustine 20, 37
  Augustine (BIDDLE) 3
  Belinda 25
  Benjamin 11
  Edward 6, 54
  Elisabeth 4, 22, 40
  Elizabeth 14, 20
  Ephraim 40, 42
  Horatio 14
  John 52
  Joshua 3, 14, 20, 37
  Leah 14
  Margaret 25
  Mary 25, 42
  Michael 22
  Nancy 37
  Penelope 22, 52
  Rebecca 14
  Sarah 25
  Shadrack 25
  Susanna 40, 42
  Susanna (WILSON) 6
  Thomas 4
  William 11, 25
RUTLIDGE, Ephraim 8
RYAN, Charlotte 36
  John Mead 36
  Joshua 36
SADLER, Elisabeth 28
  Elisabeth (HOWARD) 4
  Frances 28
  Mary Ann 28
  Thomas 4, 28
SAMPSON, 54
  Abraham 34
  Anna 41
  Elijah 13, 38, 41, 42
  Elisabeth 34, 38, 41, 42
  Emanuel 14
  Margaret 14
  Mary 10, 13, 14
  Nancy 2
  Nicholas 10
  Rachel 42
  Thomas 10
SAMSON, Aquila 2
  David 16
  Elizabeth 16

SAMSON, Isaac 16
  Mary (INLOWS) 2
  Rachel 11
  Richard 11
  Ruth 11
SANDERS, Charity 2
SANDERSONS, Maria 3
SANDIFORD, Delea (HUTCHINGS) 7
  John 7
SATER, Sarah 6
SAWYER, Edmond 27
  Mary 27
  William 27
SCALF, Barton 13
  John 13
SCARBROUGH, Arsbel 17
  James 17
  John 17
  Mary 5, 15, 17
  Samuel 15, 17
  Sarah 15
  William 17
SCARF, Hannah 25
  John 25
  Mary Fullerton 25
SCARFF, Henry 52
SCHARFF, Rebecca 7
SCHREADER, Elisabeth Johnson 33
  Jacob 33, 37
  Jacob D.S. 37
  Mary 33, 37
SCOFIELD, Mary 1
SCOGINGS, John 18, 28
  Margaret 18, 28
  Penelope 28
  William 18
SCOTT, Benjamin Colegate 26
  Colegate 11
  Daniel 5
  Elisabeth 5
  Hannah (NORRIS) 4
  Joseph 4
  Margaret (SHORT) 5
  Mary 11, 20, 26
  Nathan 11, 20, 26
  Ruth 20
SCROGGINS, Elizabeth 13
  John 13
SEDDON, George 16
  James 16
  Mary 16
SEDGWICK, Benjamin 1, 10, 20, 39
  John 10
  Mary (ALBERT) 1
  Rachel 39

SEDGWICK, Salina 10
  Selinah 39
SEMMES, William 52
SEWEL, Bazzel 20
  Elizabeth 20
  John 20
SHARP, Betsey Ann 25
  George 13
  Horatio 25
  James Eliott 25
  Marth 13   :
  Rachel 25
  Thomas 25
  William 13
SHAW, David 16
  Elesiana 38
  Elisabeth 38
  Elizabeth 12
  Joshua 12, 38
  Nicholas 12
  Rachel 16
  Rebecca 16
SHEARWOOD, Elisabeth 5
  Sarah 5
SHEETS, Joseph 43
  Ruth 43, 54
  Ruth Caroline 43
  Thomas Owings 43
SHEETZ, Joseph 6
  Ruth (OWINGS) 6
SHEPHARD, Elisabeth 25
  Hannah 12, 25
  Mary 12
  Nathaniel 12, 25
SHEPHERD, John 49
SHEPPARD,   53
SHEREDINE, Ann (ALLEN) 7
  Ann (NEILL) 5
  Anne 32
  Elisabeth 25
  James 25, 31
  John 7, 32
  Mary 5, 31
  Ruth 31
  Thomas 5, 32
SHIPLEY, Adam 6
  Benjamin 12
  Christopher 13
  Keturah 13
  Ruth (CRISMAN) 6
  Samuel 12, 13
  Thomas 13
SHOCK, John Norris 37
  Mary 35
  Peter 35

SHOCK, William 35
SHORES, John 18
  Margaret 18
  Richard 18
  Sarah 18
SHORT, Margaret 5
SHOUDY, Rachel 2
SHREEVE, Asina 53
SILK, James 28
  John 28
  Mary 28
  Nancy 28
SIMMONS, Mary 53
SINGLETON, Elisabeth 40
  John 40
  Martha 40
  Nancy 40
  Phebe 40
  Thomas 40
  William 40
SLADE,   51, 52
  Abraham 13
  Amanda Azana 44
  Armarellen 46
  Armarllon 46
  Catharine 34
  Dixon 32, 40, 45
  Edward 32
  Elisabeth 32, 34, 35, 40, 43,
    44, 45
  Elisabeth (HUTCHINGS) 6
  Elizabeth 13
  Ezekiel 46
  Independent 45
  Isaac Whidiker 18
  J. 53
  James 13
  James Whittaker 23
  John 6, 43, 44
  Josias 27, 34
  Levi 34
  Luch Smith 27
  Mary 43
  Mathida 32
  Matilda 13
  Micajah 14
  Minerva 13
  Nancy 46
  Penelope 4, 35, 45
  Priscilla 23
  Rachel 9, 14, 18
  Rebecca Ball 27
  Sally Ann 43
  Thomas 9, 14, 18, 34
  Washington 32

85

STANDIFORD, William 34, 49
STANSBURY, Abraham 12, 19, 26,
  33
  Daniel 12
  David 12
  Edmond 53
  Eleanor 27
  Elijah 13, 24
  Elisabeth 19, 24, 26, 33
  Elizabeth 12, 13
  Frances 43
  H. 52
  Heneritta 12
  Isaac 13
  Jacob 12, 24
  James Edwards 33
  Jesse 13
  John Ensor 33
  Mary 33
  Mary Slade 27
  Penelope 49
  Ruth Edwards 19, 33
  Ruth James Edward 26
  Samuel 43
  Susanna 3
  William 43
STARR, Ann 41
  James 41
STERRET, James Riel 13
STERRETT, Alexander 16
  Elizabeth 16
  William 16
STEVINSON, Andrew 4
  Isabella (SMITH) 4
STEWARD, Alexander 9
  Eleanor (DYNES) 1
  Elizabeth 9, 18
  Elizabeth (GUYTON) 1
  Henry Guyton 18
  James 1
  John 9
  William 1, 18, 51
STEWART, John 8
STOCKDALE, Sarah (BAXTER) 5
  Thomas 5
STONE, Martha Burrows 6
  William 52
STOVER, Achsah 27, 41
  Elisabeth 27
  Jacob 27, 41
  Sophia 41
  Susanna 41
STRAND, Clary 12
  Mary 12
  Thomas 12

STRANGE, Flora 17
  James 17
STRAWBRIDGE, Barbara 28
  Isaac 28
  Martha 28
STREET, Aberilla 42
  Abraham 30
  Catharine 34, 36, 40, 42
  Catharine (MERRYMAN) 7
  Charlotte 24
  David 23, 24, 28, 30, 33, 34,
    37, 39, 40, 45
  Edward Rigby 39
  Elisabeth 36
  Glenn 28, 36
  Hannah 23, 24, 28, 30, 33, 34,
    37, 39, 40, 45
  Isabella 23
  James 10
  Jefferson 40
  Jemima 11, 36
  Jemmima 24
  Jesse 11
  John 11, 24, 45
  Maria 37
  Martha 24
  Mary 11, 33
  Rachel 36
  Robert 40
  Roger 40
  Rogers 34, 36, 42
  Samuel 36
  Sarah 24, 36, 37
  Sarah Lorrinsa 34
  Sinclair 24
  Thomas 7, 10, 11, 24, 36, 37,
    52
  Thomas Corben 34
STREETT, Belinda 47
  Catharine 47
  Jane 47
  Nancy 47
  Rogers 47
STRICKLAND, Alice (PERRY) 4
  John 4
STROUD, Ann 17
  Elizabeth 9
  Harriett 9
  Mary 9, 17
  Rachel 9
  Thomas 9, 17
STUMP, Martha Burrows (STONE) 6
  Samuel 6
SUDDEN, Aquila 22
  James 22

SUDDEN, Mary 22
SUTTEN, Elizabeth 12
  Henry 12
SUTTON, Ann 38
  Benjamin 35
  Benjamin Almony 46
  Dorcas 44
  Henry 19, 38, 53
  Joseph 39, 53, 55
  Mary 19, 35, 38, 39, 40, 42, 44
  Micajah 45
  Mordicai 45
  Nancy 45
  Nicholas 40
  Prudence 46
  Ruth 38
  Thomas 35, 39, 40, 42, 44
  William 19
SWAIN, Edward 9
  Jane 9
  Rachel 9
SWANN, Federick 50
  Susanne 4
SWARTH, Sarah 2
SYKES, Ann 6
SYMILEAR, Lester 50
SYNCLEAR, Bailey 10
  Elizabeth 9
  James 10, 12, 28
  Jane 12
  Lester 9
  Thomas 28
TALBOTT, Ann 3
  Belinda 28
  Edmond 50
  Eliabeth 53
  Elisabeth 28, 35
  Elisabeth (RUTLEDGE) 4
  Mary 4, 35
  Mary (MERRYMAN) 6
  Thomas 4, 6, 28, 35
TALLEY, 53
TALLY, Martha Susanne 4
TAYLOR, Andrew 17
  Catharine 17
  Charlotte 2
  Clemency (THOMSON) 1
  Corban 18
  Elisabeth 5
  Elizabeth 17, 18
  Hannah 50
  James 18
  John 18
  Moses 3
  Nancy (DURBAN) 3

TAYLOR, Richard 1
TAYSON, (Widow) 37
  Cassandra 37
  Elijah 37
  Elisabeth 37
  Mary 37
THOMAS, John 51
  Mary 54
  Ralph 55
THOMSON, Alexander 10, 13
  Ann 10
  Clemency 1
  Elizabeth 10
  John 10
  Lusby 10
  Moses 10
  Priscilla 13
  Sarah 13
THORN, Sarah (SATER) 6
  William 6
THRAP, Mary 1
TIBBITT, Delilah 33
  Elisabeth 33
  Joshua 33
  Walter 33
TIBITT, Belilah 13
  Rebecca 13
  Walter 13
TIMANUS, 53
TODD, Elizabeth 17
  Patrick 17
  Sabrai 17
TOLBY, Abby 9
  Elizabeth 9
  Zephaniah 9
TOLLEY, Abby 9
  Elizabeth 9, 52
  Zephaniah 9
TOOGOOD, Sy 18
  William 18
TOWNSLEY, John 9
  Joseph 9
  Margaret 9
TOWSON, Abednigo 37
  Charlotte 16
  Elisabeth 37
  Frances 11, 16
  James 11
  Joshua 37
  Mary 37
  Obadiah 11
  Obediah 16
TRACY, Isiah 12
  Noty 12
  Warral 12

TRAPNALL, Nancy 5
TRAPNELL, William 51
TREACY, John 12
  Rebecca 12
  William 12
TRONER, Jane 10
  Sarah 10
  William 10
TUCK, Cassandra 14
  Catharine 14
  Elizabeth 14
  Esau 14
  James 14
  John 14
  Martha 14
TUDER, Joshua 3
  Polley 3
  Salathiel 3
  Susannah (MCCUBBINS) 3
  Temperance (FUGATE) 3
TURK, Catharine 22
  Esau 22
  George 22
TURNBULL, Robert 2
  Sarah (BUCKANAN) 2
TURNER, Aquila 40
  Jamima 40
  Nancy 2
  Thomas 40
TURNPAW, Hannah 14
  John 14
  Mary 14
TWIBLE, Elisabeth 32
  John 32
  Martha 32
TWYBLE, David 22
  Elisabeth 22
  John 22
TYDINGS, Richard 5
  Susanna (CHAMBERLAIN) 5
TYSON, George 42
  Mary 34, 38, 40, 42
  Rachel 40
  Richard 38
  William 34, 38, 40, 42
VANCE, Mary (WATTERS) 5
  Samuel 5
VANHORN, Benjamin 2
  Charity (SANDERS) 2
VAUGHAN, Abraham 41, 44, 45, 47
  Benjamin 42, 45, 54
  Elisabeth 38, 41
  Elizabeth 53
  Gest 47, 52
  Gist 44, 47

VAUGHAN, James 47
  John 38
  Rachel 3, 38, 41, 42, 44, 45, 47
  Rebecca Gott 42
VAUGHN, Charlotte 47
  Emmaline 47
  Gest 47
  Thomas Norris 47
WADLEY, Hannah 11
  Samuel 11
  Solomon 54
WADSWORTH, James 36, 40
  John 25
  Lydia 36, 40
  Sarah 25
  Thomas 36
  Thomas Dunkin 25
WAGGONER, Barbary 37
  Jacob 37, 54
  Ruth 37
WAITS, Susanna (STANSBURY) 3
  William Wilkinson 3
WALKER, Catharine 15
  Daniel 35
  Elizabeth 15
  George 15
  Jimmima 15
  Joseph 15
  Margaret 53
  Mary 35
  Prudence 35
  Richard 15
WALLER, Bazzel 10
  Mary 10
  Sarah 10
WALLIS, Cassandra (JOLLEY) 4
  Samuel 4
WALSH, Blanch (LEE) 2
  William 2
WALTER, Ann (DELANY) 2
  Thomas 2
WALTHAM, Thomas 5
WALTON, Abel 48
  Ann 48
  Dinah 48
  Jane 48
WANE, John 49
WARD, Ann 11, 16
  Ann Colegate 16
  Elizabeth 10
  James 10, 11, 16, 49
  Jane 40, 42
  John 10, 40
  Joseph 40, 42

WARD, Margaret 10
  Martha 10
  Martha (BEWARD) 1
  Richard 1
  Widow 52
  William 11, 42
WARE, Abraham 47
  Benjamin 14
  Mary 47
  Rebecca 14
  Ruth 47
  Thomas 14, 53
WARRICK, Elisabeth 24
  Jermey 24
  John 24
WARRICKE, Elizabeth 17
  John 17
  Thomas 17
WATE, Diana 30
  Richard 30
WATERS, Elisabeth 5
  Godfrey 1
  Grace (WILSON) 3
  Henry 3
  Martha 2
  Martha (BRADFORD) 1
  Sarah 2
WATKINS, Elisabeth (ALDRIDGE) 7
  John 5
  Ruth (GUYTON) 5
  Samuel 51
  Sarah 1
  Vincent Jeoffrey 7
WATT, Ann 39
  David 36
  Elizabeth 11
  James 10
  John 39
  Nancey 24
  Robert 10, 11, 24, 36, 39
  Sarah 10, 11, 24, 36, 39
  William 36
WATTERS, Mary 5
WEAR, Charity (KEY) 2
  James 2
WEATHERALL, Charlotte E. (DAY) 5
  Henry 5
  Mary (PRESBURY) 5
  William 5
WEBB, Belinda 18, 34
  Elisabeth 26
  Isaac 18
  Margaret 34
  Percy 15
  Samuel 11, 15, 18, 26, 34

WEBSTER, James 21
  Mary 21
  Susanna 21
WEEKS, Ann 15, 17
  John 15, 17
  Lucretia 1
  Mary 15
  Sarah 1, 17
WELCH, Martha (GROVES) 4
  Thomas 4
WELLS, Thomas 54
WEST, Ann 13
  Gassaway 41
  James 13
  Luke 41
  Martha 13
  Mary 13
  Sarah 41
  Sybel 5
  Thomas 13
WETHERALL, George Henry 40
  Mary 40
  William 40
WHEELER, Ann 35, 36
  Anna 30
  Ariel 42
  Charlotte 10
  Delilah 36
  Elizabeth 16
  George 30
  Joseph Stansbury 36
  Josias 1
  Kitty 30
  Martha 16, 50
  Martha (PRIGG) 1
  Mary 30
  Ruth 30
  Sarah 16, 28, 30, 36, 42
  Stephen 36
  Temperance 36
  Thomas 10
  Wann 36
  Wason 16, 28, 30
  Wasten 42
  William 30, 35
WHEGERS, John Henry 48
  Mary 48
  Rebecca 48
WHITACRE, John 12
  Lauson Mackee 12
  Rachel 12
WHITAKER, John 9
  Rachel 9
  Susanna 1
WHITE, Deliah 5

WHITE, Hannah (BULL) 5
James 5
WHITEFORD, Nancy (MCCAIRNAN) 5
Robert 5
WHITTAKER, John 51
WICORT, Andrew 53
WIER, Comfort 45
Eveline 45
Henry 45
WILEY, 55
Andrew 40
Ann 23
Hugh 23
John Stephenson 15
Joseph 40
Joshua Cooper 40
Mary 23
Sarah 15, 40
Vincent 15
William 15
WILIE, Ann (RICKETS) 6
John 6
WILLIAMS, Ann Yellott 42, 54
Catharine 41
Christana 42
Daniel 44
Eleanor 42
Ely 44
Hannah Yellott 43
John 3, 44
Joshua 41
Mary 42, 43
Peacy 44
Rachel (VAUGHAN) 3
Rice 42
Robert 42, 43
Sarah 42
Thomas 41
WILLITT, Michael 54
WILMER, Anna (FORD) 6
William 6
WILMOT, Hannah 1
Mary 6
WILMOTT, Mary 49
WILSON, Andrew 7, 47
Ann 30
Bethia 23
Charlotte 28
Deliah 32
Delilah 15, 23, 28
Edward 32
Gaum 32
Gavin 23
Gideon 54
Gittings 21

WILSON, Grace 3
Gwin 15, 28
Henry 4
James 47
Jane 21
John 30
Joseph 30
Josias 48
Lily 15
Martha 37
Mary 30
R. 47
Rebecca (SCHARFF) 7
Sarah (WORTHINGTON) 4
Sarah Chew (LEE) 5
Susanna 6
William 50
William Lee 5
WINCHESTER, James 38
Samuel 38
Sarah 38
WINE, Comfort 42
Henry 42
Mary Ann 42
WINGATE, Sarah (POTTEE) 4
Thomas 4
WIRES, Comfort 47
WITHERAL, James 26
Sarah 26
William 26
WODSWORTH, Jannet 38
Mary Ann 38
Sarah 38
Thomas 38
WOLF, Michael 52
WOOD, Achsah 19
Sarah 19
WOODLAND, James 3
Sarah (COLLINS) 3
WORREL, Mary (CONDEN) 1
Thomas 1
WORTHINGTON, Ann Lee (FITZHUGH)
7
Brice John 7
Charles 6, 7
Charlotte 6
Hannah (YELLOTT) 7
Sarah 4, 7
Susanna (JOHNS) 6
WRIGHT, Ann 28, 31, 51
Ann (GREEN) 2
George 27
Harry 28, 51
John 2
Joshua 31

WRIGHT, Patty 27
  Rachel 27
  Rebecca 49
  Rebecca (OTHARSON) 2
  Thomas 2, 28, 31, 51
WYLE, Charlotte 41, 43
  Joshua 43
  Luke 41, 43
  Thomas 41
YARLEY, Mehala 27
  Ralph 5, 27
  Rebecca 5, 27
  Ruth (BURTON) 5
YEISER, Eleanor A. (HOLLIDAY) 6
  John 6
YELLOT, Elisabeth 44
  John 44
  Rebecca R. 44
YELLOTT, Bethia 46

YELLOTT, Charles 48
  Coleman 48
  Elisabeth 48
  George 46, 48
  Hannah 7
  J. 48
  Jeremiah 46, 48
  John 7, 44, 46, 48
  John Jeremiah 46
  Mary 44, 48
  R. R. 48
  Rebecca R. 44, 46, 47, 48
  Rebecca R. (COLEMAN) 7
  Thomas 48
  W. 48
  Washington 48
  William 46
YOUNG, Clara 4
  Hugh 52

Heritage Books by Martha and Bill Reamy:

*Erie County, New York Obituaries as Found in the Files
of the Buffalo and Erie County Historical Society*

Genealogical Abstracts from Biographical and Genealogical
History of the State of Delaware, *Volumes 1 and 2*

History and Roster of Maryland Volunteers, War of 1861–1865: Index

Immigrant Ancestors of Marylanders, as Found in Local Histories

Pioneer Families of Orange County, New York

*Records of St. Paul's Parish, [Baltimore, Maryland]
Volumes 1 and 2*

St. George's Parish Register [Harford County, Maryland], 1689–1793

St. James Parish Registers, 1787–1815

St. Thomas' Parish Registers, 1732–1850

The Index of Scharf's History of Baltimore City and County *[Maryland]*

Heritage Books by Martha Reamy:

*1860 Census Baltimore City: Volume 1, 1st and 2nd Wards
(Fells Point and Canton Waterfront Areas)*

Abstracts of Carroll County Newspapers, 1831–1846
Marlene Bates and Martha Reamy

Abstracts of South Central Pennsylvania Newspapers: Volume 2, 1791–1795

*Early Church Records of Chester County, Pennsylvania,
Volume 1: Bradford Monthly Meeting*

Early Church Records of Chester County, Pennsylvania, Volume 2
Martha Reamy and Charlotte Meldrum

Early Church Records of Chester County, Pennsylvania, Volume 3

Early Families of Otsego County, New York, Volume 1